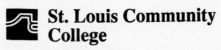

St. Louis Community College

Forest Park
Florissant Valley
Meramec

Instructional Resources
St. Louis, Missouri

D1126509

Transforming the Cinderella Dream

Transforming the Cinderella Dream

❧   ❧   ❧

FROM FRANCES BURNEY TO CHARLOTTE BRONTË

Huang Mei

RUTGERS UNIVERSITY PRESS

New Brunswick and London

*The research for this volume was supported in part by the
David L. Kalston Memorial Fund, Rutgers University.*

Library of Congress Cataloging-in-Publication Data

Huang Mei, 1950–
    Transforming the Cinderella dream : from Frances Burney to
Charlotte Brontë / Huang Mei.
        p.   cm.
    Based on the author's Ph.D. dissertation, Rutgers University.
    Includes bibliographical references.
    ISBN 0-8135-1522-X
    1. English fiction—Women authors—History and criticism.
2. Cinderella (Legendary character) in literature.   3. Fairy tales—
Adaptations—History and criticism.   4. Women and literature—Great
Britain.   5. Folklore in literature.   6. Women in literature.
    I. Title
PR830.C527M45   1990
823.009'27'082—dc20
                                                          89-39326
                                                          CIP

British Cataloging-in-Publication information available

CONTENTS

PREFACE

The present book is rooted in my personal encounter with a foreign culture. I joined the Graduate English Program of Rutgers University in 1983, being one of the thousands of Chinese students who have carried on their studies in Western universities after China recently reopened its "door" to the world. Immersed for the first time in a very alien environment, I became increasingly self-conscious about my Chinese mental makeup. I was struck by the overwhelming way that the mythical, legendary, and religious elements have dominated a nation's literary imagination, through people's semi-instinctive choices in such things as vocabulary, image, metaphor, archetype, and narrative pattern. And the English novel up to the late nineteenth century, in comparison with the French or Russian ones, seems to have very zealously followed the fairy tale structure, with the predictable happy ending.

I have been particularly fascinated by the ever-present passive and innocent heroine in the English novels patterned on Cinderella, and by the noticeable difference between the archetypal woman image in these works and in Chinese folklore. I remember vividly that during my first semester at Rutgers, in a class on the Romantics, I remarked that Keats's phantasmagoric Lamia called to mind another snake woman—the legendary brave and humane Madame White Snake in an extremely popular Chinese folk tale. It is true that in some other Chinese folk tales, as well as in certain versions of "The Legend of the White Snake," the snake woman is glamorous yet dangerously sinister. However, as Chen Jian-xian, a young Chinese folklorist, points out, unlike the Western tales, which usually present the snake woman as evil and monstrous, the Oriental tradition (Chinese and Indian) more often conceives of her as a good fairy. In the now better known version, both Madame White Snake and her maid, Little Blue (Snake), are beautiful, courageous, and indeed very lovable. Intriguingly, in many Chinese folk tales and literary works the positive women figures display unusual strength, courage, and initiative. Of the four greatest Chinese folk tales, three—"The Legend of the White Snake," "Meng Jiang, the Woman Whose Crying Shattered the Great Wall," and "Liang Shan-bo and Zhu Ying-tai"—have women as the central figures and the chief actors. In the other one, "The Story of the Shepherd Boy and the Weaving Girl," the heroine is at least as active as the male protagonist. This is also true of many literary works, especially *The Stories from the Lodge of Leisure* by P'u Sung-ling (1640–1715), which have been generally accepted and appreciated by the educated people, if not exactly by the moral and ideological authorities of the time. Usually it is the simple-minded, poor, peasant boy or the shiftless scholar rather than the Sleeping Beauty who dreams of a magic lover/ rescuer of the opposite sex. If, as some feminists assert, the stories about docile girls like the Sleeping Beauty, Snow White, or Cinderella help to "perpetuate the patriarchal status quo by making female subordination seem a romantically desirable, indeed an inescapable fate" (Rowe, "Feminism and Fairy Tales" 237), how can we explain the fact that a more rigidly structured and oppressively patriarchal society like that of ancient China produced a lively and disruptive archetype like Madame White Snake?[1]

Once I mentioned this difference casually to a young folklorist, Mary Ellen Cohane, then at Rutgers. She asked me: "Do you know that the Cinderella story might have come from China?" I was astonished. For me, as for millions of Chinese common readers, Cinderella comes in a Walt Disney cartoon costume and is a totally Western creature.

My curiosity was further aroused, and once I started reading more on the subject, my list of Cinderellas grew rapidly. It seems that since Richardson's Pamela triumphantly married her rakish master, an impressively large number of literary heroines (mostly created by female hands) has followed in the wake of that demure servant-maid. Invariably we have a homeless or partly homeless girl successfully pass her trials and marry into financial security and a higher social station. Those relatively obscure names like Lucy Wellers, Henrietta Courtney, Caroline Asford, Juliana,[2] or even Belinda and Evelina, may escape a modern reader, yet anyone who reads in English literature is almost sure to come across some of Jane Austen's marriageable girls or Charlotte Brontë's strong-willed little governesses. Given the fact that "the earliest datable version of the Cinderella story anywhere in the world occurs in a Chinese book written about 850–860 A.D." (Waley 226), why has it remained so very marginal in Chinese culture,[3] yet gained so conspicuous a place in the mainstream of English literature? What is its special appeal to the eighteenth-century English mind, and to women in particular? And why did the Cinderella plot become so problematic by the mid-nineteenth century—rather soon after its heyday—that the future bridegroom in *Villette* is dismissed just before the last page, and that punishment is meted out to every dreaming cinder girl in George Eliot's novels?

Such reflections have led to further probing into the actual formation and transformation of the Cinderella theme in the works of English novelists and resulted in this present book. It is not a comparative literary study, since I decided to concentrate on a group of British women writers (I will discuss my reason for choosing these specific writers later on) and to keep my Chinese perspectives firmly in the background. Neither will it be an archetypal study. My intention is to trace the development of this popular narrative pattern through close textual studies of the individual novels. The emphasis will be on the differences, on the unique ways each writer tries to manipulate and reshape the convention—and the literary or nonliterary implications of such attempts—rather than on the archetypal resemblances those works bear to the original fairy tale or to the established narrative paradigm. In this context the book might perhaps better be termed a "historical" study.

By using the term "historical," I do not mean to trap myself in the theoretical snarl about the problematic "reality" outside the text, which is so much challenged by current Western criticism. From my vantage point, the "adventure" of the Cinderella plot in English culture, which is so very different from its historical lot in China, is obviously not only decided by the linguistic or literary interplay within the tale itself, but also by its complicated relation to the nation's economic, social, and cultural life. These chapters will not go into what we usually call "history" in detail, but I would like to suggest that the mutations and vicissitudes the Cinderella theme has undergone are in one way or another connected to the "actual" life and to the consciousness of the people of the time.

Needless to say, my study, partly because of its subject, is very much indebted to feminist critical practice. And since feminist criticism is itself very much a theoretical arena, it is only natural that my relation to various opinions in this "school" is one of continuous dialogue, even argument, which I find both inspiring and invigorating.

ACKNOWLEDGMENTS

This study is based on my dissertation work. It was made possible by the joint financial support from the English Department, Rutgers University, the Chinese National Committee of Education, and Harvard Yenching Institute, which enabled me to complete my doctoral study at Rutgers University. I want to thank all of the professors, classmates, and friends in the United States who have contributed, directly or indirectly, to my study, among whom are those names forever dear to me: Bridget Lyons, Donald Stone, Linda Kozusko, Caroline Huber. I am especially indebted to the advisers on my dissertation committee, George Levine, Barry Qualls, and Bruce Robbins, as well as my editors Leslie Mitchner, Eve Pearson, and Marilyn Campbell, whose inspiring suggestions, critical comments, and careful corrections have helped me to write and rewrite the book into its present shape.

I would also like to take the opportunity to express my heartfelt gratitude to my family and my colleagues in the Institute of Foreign Literature, Chinese Academy of Social Sciences, without whose unremitting support I could not have begun my study in the United States more than five years ago, nor ever been able to complete it.

Transforming the Cinderella Dream

Introduction:
Cinderella as the Paragon

> I wish I could—, I wish I could—; she could not speak the
> rest, her tears interrupting her. Her godmother, who
> was a Fairy, said to her, Thou wishest thou could'st go to
> the ball, is it not so? Y—es, said Cinderella, with a great
> sob.
>
> —"Cinderella: or, The Little
> Glass Slipper"

R. P. Utter and G. B. Needham, who claim "every heroine
in fiction" is "a daughter of Pamela" (1), comment on the
origin of *Pamela*'s narrative scheme: "if Richardson had known
all the folk literature of the world, and had deliberately searched
it, he could hardly have chosen a more popular theme. It is
the fairy tale of the type we name for its best known heroine,
Cinderella" (329). J.M.S. Tompkins also remarks about how
the potboiling narratives of the late eighteenth century learned
from Richardson "to dress up the old theme of Cinderella, Virtue Persecuted" (34).

Indeed, "Cinderella" is one of the most convenient tags to cat-
egorize a heroine and her "story." Michael Adelstein (28) and
Kristina Straub (43, 154, 164) attach it to the plot elements in
Frances Burney's writing; Annis Pratt applies it to Mrs. Smith's
novels (26–27); Tony Tanner (10) and D. W. Harding ("Introduction to *Persuasion*" 24; "Regulated Hatred" 73) connect it
with Austen's protagonists; Karen Rowe (" 'Fairy-born' " 72),
Richard Chase (469), and Gilbert and Gubar (342) refer to this
widely circulated term in discussing Jane Eyre. And Mary Scrutton groups together several famous heroines—from Pamela to
Fanny Price—and labels them all "bourgeois Cinderellas" (351).

Unlike these casual references, which presuppose the reader's familiarity with the fairy tale and give no further definition of the term "Cinderella," the present study takes the Cinderella pattern seriously, both as a favorite narrative paradigm in the English novel, and as an illuminating interpretive key. Such a critical enterprise demands, of course, a closer examination of the fairy tale itself. As "the best-known fairy-story in the world," "Cinderella" has some seven hundred variants (Opie and Opie 117, 121). In her comprehensive study, *Cinderella: Three Hundred and Forty-Five Variants,* Marian R. Cox points out that the two features essential to all Cinderella tales are an initially "ill-treated heroine" and her eventual "recognition by means of shoe" (xxv). Simple as they are, these two features set down the basic pattern of narrative development, which forms the most frequently used plot for a female protagonist in the English novel and is often vaguely referred to as "the romance," "the love plot," or "the courtship plot." These two features, then, can be seen as the distinctive trademark of the novels in this line.

In the present study the term "Cinderella" refers specifically to the tale retold by Perrault, who gave the story the form in which it is known throughout the world today. It first appeared in 1697 and was soon collected in his *Histoires ou contes du temps passé* (1697), a book better known for its alternative title, *Tales of My Mother Goose (Contes de ma mere l'oye).* Robert Sambers "transplanted" it to England in 1729, just before the first bloom of the English novel. From that time on, Perrault's "Cinderella" gradually established itself as the standard version in English and became a regular part of the "staple fare in the nursery" (Kramnick 213).

Perrault's story belongs to what Jack Zipes calls "the literary fairy tales," which, as he emphasizes, came into being with the emerging bourgeois society and were in many ways fundamentally different from "the folktale," which was rooted in the pre-capitalistic lower-class culture (*Fairy Tales* 6–11). There are several things about Perrault's revisioning that are worth consideration. The first is that he Christianized the tale. In some other versions—for example, in the Brothers Grimm's—there are more violent elements and the heroine is by far less submissive than Perrault's Cinderella (Opie and Opie 118; Bettelheim

251). Perrault's heroine, degraded to do "the meanest work," to dress in "poor clothes" and stay in ashes, not only "bore all patiently" (123) without any visible resentment, but "offered herself" to help her spoiled stepsisters prepare for the grand ball. Toward the end of the story, when she is identified as the "beautiful lady" sought by the prince, she still takes no opportunity to avenge her wrongs, but embraces her discomfited sisters and tells them that she forgives them with all her heart. This does not mean, as Bruno Bettelheim assumes, that "it does not make all that much difference whether one is vile or virtuous" (252). On the contrary, by enduring injustice patiently and returning ill-usage with love and benevolence, this Cinderella transforms her passive innocence and suffering into a saving power, which earns her a "happily-ever-after"ending and converts her world from a house of petty cruelty into a harmonious, merry court. In her unrivaled humbleness, patience, and kindness, she is very much an incarnation of positive Christian virtues.

Remarkably, in Perrault's tale, the Christian godmother has replaced all the pantheist helpers—trees, fish, birds, or cows—that we meet in many other versions. Although the actual function of this fairy godmother is not very different from that of a bird or a cow, the change carefully circumscribes Cinderella's life within the Christian world. In the "Second Moral" that concludes the tale, Perrault teaches the importance of "godmothers." This indicates how self-conscious he is when deciding the identity of the magic helper, no matter whether he is fully serious or half-mocking with that "Moral."

With the intensification of the Christian quality of the heroine, the meaning of the tiny slipper shifts considerably as well. It is true that in many languages the word "shoe" or "slipper" has a strong sexual connotation (Bettelheim 265, 269). But in this tale it is an emblem more of Cinderella's true identity as a noble lady than of her adolescent sexuality. The size and beauty of the slipper imply a delicate physique and an elegant style that are usually related to upper-class female life. Also embedded in the long history of the verbal image of shoe/slipper is a specific moral nuance. Because the ancient Chinese "Cinderella" has been found to be the earliest one, it might be helpful to take into account the high prestige enjoyed by small foot size in the old Chinese culture; this was the result of the highly polarized sex role in the upper classes and ended in the notorious convention of foot-binding among women.[1] Choosing a wife solely or mainly on the ground of the size of her feet was not an uncommon practice. A pair of perfectly bound small feet became the symbol of a fragile feminine beauty, as well as of the highest female virtue—for it marked the woman's obedience to the existing order and promised her future dependence on man. In the context of the underlined patience and obedience of the heroine, this patriarchal suggestion in regard to the ideal of female perfection is obviously what Perrault has deliberately picked up when he chooses to place a tiny slipper in the center of the narrative as the only token of Cinderella's true identity. The authorial accent does not, of course, completely banish other meanings from the field of signification, but it can partially control the signifying process and give the image of the slipper a Christian overtone.

The second point I want to mention here about Perrault's "Cinderella" is its puzzling textual complexity and ambiguity, which stand out strikingly in spite of the authorial effort to integrate the text with Christian morality. People often juxtapose Cinderella with Snow White or the Sleeping Beauty without differentiating among these archetypes of the passive and submissive woman. Simone de Beauvoir is rather typical in this respect when she says in *The Second Sex* that "Woman is the Sleeping Beauty, Cinderella, Snow White, she who receives and submits" (328). This is, however, an inaccurate observation. Perrault's Cinderella, though apparently more passive than other of her sister cinder girls, does express her will and take the initiative at the crucial points of her life. Notably, it is her crying that calls forth her godmother, whose existence has not been hinted at before. She sobs out her inchoate discontent and desire in front of that fairy protector and obtains the needed outfit to go to the ball. Later, when the slipper test is going on in her house, she once again recognizes the opportunity and speaks to royal envoys: "Let me see if it will not fit me" (127). On both occasions Cinderella is active, rather than passive, and forges her own lot.

Her behavior after her first sensational appearance at the ball is even more perplexing. Having managed to get home before her stepsisters, she goes to the door to meet them, "gaping, rubbing her eyes, and stretching herself," and chatters with them about the mysterious lady at the ball: "She must then be very handsome indeed; Lord how happy have you been, could not I see her? Ah! good Madam Charlotte, lend me your yellow suit of clothes that you wear every day" (126). Even allowing for her justifiable wish to keep the secret and avoid probable harm, there is absolutely no need for such inventive and self-pleased improvising. At this moment she looks more a born actress and an experienced schemer than a submissive heroine. This difference from the Sleeping Beauty, who essentially does nothing except sleep and dream, is important and points to the central paradox of the tale: on the one hand, the heroine is praised for her humility, her patience and self-effacement; yet on the other hand, all the vivid details hint at a longing and plotting girl, one who is the necessary underside of the Christianized heroine. With her partly suppressed and partly suggested wishes (as conveyed by the broken sentence "I wish I could—") coming true in the end, that aspiring girl is ultimately affirmed and supported by the narrative structure. We shall see in the subsequent discussions how this ambiguous pattern lends itself readily to the novelistic imagination, and how women novelists, with special eagerness and anxiety, respond to this structuring paradox of the Cinderella theme.

A few more words about the (step)mother-daughter relationship would be pertinent here. In some older versions there is sometimes an "unnatural father" who wants to marry his daughter, and, being angry at her resistance, expels her in a King Lear manner. During the evolution of the story, the motif of the "unnatural father" gradually vanishes, and the relation with the cruel stepmother and stepsisters is foregrounded. This emphasis on the stepmother has its historical basis in the social life of the time. According to Robert Darnton, because of the high mortality rate and frequent remarriage of widowed men (remarriage is relatively rarer among widowed women), "stepmothers proliferated everywhere" in eighteenth-century rural

France (27). Of course, the final selection of a mother as the parental figure in folklore perhaps owes more to the sociopsychological effect of the gender arrangement of human family. Hitherto in most civilized cultures, the woman has been the main caretaker of the child, and consequently by far the major object of the child's ambivalence.[2] This "female monopoly of early child care" (Dinnerstein 33) became even more overwhelming with the emergence of the middle-class nuclear family, to which we may connect, I believe, the amazing frequency with which a stepmother heads fairy tale families. The disappearance of the "unnatural father," then, must be viewed in the perspective of the historical changes that make the motif no longer interesting and relevant for its audience, instead of being read, as by Bettelheim, mainly as a sign that "the oedipal involvement" of the heroine has been "suppressed" (248–249). The oppressive stepmother and sisters here stand for a certain hierarchical order; and Cinderella's actual status as a servant in the household gives the introductory situation an unmistakable social connotation. With this emphasis on the master-slave relationship, the thematic tension of the tale is being formulated in a context larger and more complicated than the Freudian landscape of familial psychological interactions.[3]

There are some interesting feminist interpretations that are equally biased. In *The Madwoman in the Attic*, Gilbert and Gubar view the tale of "Snow White" as an archetypal pattern in women's writing. In their opinion, Snow White is the "patriarchy's angelic daughter" (39) who constitutes only the "surface story," and the wicked queen is the rebellious, angry woman, the active plotmaker and the artist who carries the dynamic narrative energy (3–44, 146–186). Perceptive as many of their ideas are, Gilbert and Gubar have sometimes projected too much of their interpretive intention onto the text, owing to their eagerness to redress the age-old androcentric bias in literary study as well as in social life. Typically, they read the huntsman who refuses to kill Snow White as "a surrogate for the King, a parental—or, more specifically, patriarchal—figure" (39). Such a reading, though valid in its own way, should not overshadow other interpretive possibilities. For example, the queen, in spite of her gender, can be seen as the "parental—or more specifically, patriarchal—figure," whereas the huntsman, as a servant, is consequently more sympathetic with the persecuted girl. For the young, the powerless, and the deprived, the wicked stepmother might be just the personification of oppressive authority. Though the wicked mother in a way releases a self-assertive urge, she does so chiefly by means of her position as the representative of parental authority. Perhaps this is more accurate for "Cinderella," in which the mother figure is less individualized and psychologized than in "Snow White."

Although Gilbert and Gubar's view of "Snow White" is very refreshing, it is sometimes far-fetched when applied as a universal pattern to literary works by women. After all, in classic English novels, it is the virtuous young daughter, not the evil stepmother, who occupies the spotlight. My suggestion is that the thriving tribe of apparently docile and virtuous girls is to a larger degree patterned on Cinderella, who is much more active and complex than our cursory first impression indicates. We do not have to read every wicked mother figure, such as Mrs. Norris, into an antipatriarchal subverter to discover a fermenting female consciousness and dynamic textual intricacies.

Richardson's Pamela is fully aware that she is gloriously transformed as soon as she has traded her humble name "Andrews" for the more consequential "Mrs. B." In her own words, she used to be a "poor creature" (25, 29, 69). Later she begins to talk about "the dignity" her husband has "raised" her to (424): "times . . . are much altered with me," says this newly-made lady to a servant of her insolent sister-in-law, "and I have been of late so much honoured with better company, that I can't stoop to yours" (414).

The miraculous metamorphosis is enacted, as in Cinderella's case, by marrying into a higher social class. With this young servant girl, Richardson successfully recasts the age-old tale into a popular bourgeois myth,[4] whose tenor is that a helpless girl, being "honest, though poor" (17), may eventually win love, respect, money, and everything desirable by dint of her moral superiority. Whether Perrault's text was actually known to Richardson—which is likely, considering his profession as a printer—or whether Richardson has unconsciously used this archetype makes no material difference here. The similarities between the two narratives are striking enough for people to name Pamela's story after her better known forerunner—Cinderella. That the narrative pattern was found most attractive by both Richardson and his enthusiastic middle-class readers is enough to tell its centrality to the social sensibility of the time.

Two features about the new Cinderella myth are decidedly bourgeois. One is that for a woman, perfect worldly glory and happiness no longer are attained by joining the royal family; rather, she has far more "realistic" goals—becoming a lady and gaining admission to the social club named "gentility." Secondly, the lady-to-be is distinguished mainly by her unwavering virtue and her impeccably proper behavior. If Christianized moral goodness is implied in Perrault's tale, in Richardson it is overtly and tirelessly stressed. As the finally "reformed" Mr. B confesses: "they were the beauties of her mind, that made me her *husband*" (427).

In *Pamela*, the apparent simplicity and naturalness of the fairy tale has disappeared, while its ambiguity is being acutely grasped and developed as a structuring stylistic and thematic dialectic. Distinct and conflictive discourses are ushered in, partly because of the author's didactic purpose. The cinder girl is merged with the Christian hero; the lover initially takes the voice of a Restoration rake. Between them there is a constant verbal and sexual tension, which verges on some form of catastrophe: a rape, a destruction, or a marriage. In other words, when it was transformed into a novel, the Cinderella theme, enriched and complicated, grew into "a phenomenon multiform in style and variform in speech and voice" (Bakhtin 261).

Both Pamela and Mr. B look at their lives in the light of existing literary "plots." At a sensitive point in the evolution of their relationship, Mr. B demands from Pamela her journal letters: "There is such a pretty air of romance, as you relate them, in *your* plots and *my* plots" (242). For Mr. B, the upper-class libertine, this verbal/sexual wrestling is one of the few favorite "sports" in which he can exert his wisdom and energy, and possession of a pretty virgin will certainly increase his credit and glory.[5] But "a good fame and a chastity inviolate" are Pamela's "best jewels" (198–201), her passport to respect and final salvation. Hers is a Miltonian-Bunyanesque project, as far as her conscious intention is concerned. Like Milton's Christ and Bunyan's Christian, our pious heroine has to create her identity through "trials." As Pamela's father solemnly teaches: "Temptations are sore things, but yet, without them, we know not ourselves, nor what we are able to do" (20). Pamela is fully aware of the antithetic nature of her plan and Mr. B's plan. "He may condescend," she remarks to a friendly fellow servant, "perhaps, to think I may be good enough for his harlot; and those things don't disgrace men that ruin poor women, as the world goes . . ." (36). To Mr. B she says on other occasions: "your honour is to destroy mine: and your love is to ruin mine" (218–219); and, "the honour of the wicked is disgrace and shame to the virtuous" (126–127). Even Mr. B becomes aware very early that his part in Pamela's plot is to play the "devil incarnate" (30). And Pamela the narrator open-handedly bestows on him attributes like "wicked," "base," "villainous," and "vile."

In *Paradise Regained*, the encounter between Christ and the Devil in the desert is described in terms of a war. Words with martial connotation, such as "foil, "defeat," "repulse," "debel," and "vanquish" are used when Milton describes the oppositional situation. However, this "war" between Good and Evil is essentially a battle of languages, an exhaustingly long debate. Richardson, with a perception shaped by this classical presentation of temptation, spells out the militant mission of Virtue through the voice of the "editor," for whom the attempts of the immoral rake to debauch the chaste heroine are no less than a class war in which "riches and power conspire against innocence and a low estate" (91).

This clash is an all-out Miltonian verbal battle between contending plots, languages, and styles. Though Mr. B is not allowed an equal chance in writing out his own story—as Lovelace gets in *Clarissa*—still he can be heard through Pamela's diligent recording. I will quote here as an example, one of their numerous exchanges of words; it occurs early in the novel when Mr. B has just made clear his "ignominious" intention:

if you could be so afraid of your own servants knowing of your attempts upon a poor unworthy creature, that is under your protection while I stay, surely your honour ought to be more afraid of God Almighty, in whose presence we all stand, in every action of our lives, and to whom the greatest, as well as the least, must be accountable, let them think what they list.

He took my hand, in a kind of good-humoured mockery, and said, Well urged, my pretty preacher! When my Lincolnshire chaplain dies, I'll put thee on a gown and cassock, and thou'lt make a good figure in his place.—I wish, said I, a little vexed at his jeer, your honour's conscience would be your preacher, and then you would need no other chaplain. Well, well, Pamela, said he, no more of this unfashionable jargon. . . .

Well, said he, you are an ungrateful baggage; but I am thinking it would be pity, with these fair soft hands, and that lovely skin . . . that you should return again to hard work, as you must if you go to your father's; and so I would advise her [Mrs. Jervis] to take a house in London and let lodgings to us members of parliament, when we come to town; and such a pretty daughter as you may pass for, will always fill her house, and she'll get a great deal of money.

I was sadly vexed at his barbarous joke; but being ready to cry before, the tear gushed out. . . . Why you need not take this matter in such high disdain!—You have a very pretty romantic turn for virtue, and all that. . . . But, my child (sneeringly he spoke it,) do but consider what a fine opportunity you will then have for a tale everyday to good mother Jervis, and what subjects for letter-writing to your father and mother, and what pretty preachments you may hold forth to the young gentlemen. (66–67)

The contrast of their speeches tells much about the two dialogists, and about the novel as a whole. Pamela the speaker/writer is conscientiously creating a desired verbal image for herself as a God-fearing, virtuous "poor maiden" (67). She is constantly aware of her triple listener/reader—the licentious master/lover, the strict father/judge, and the heavenly Father—the threefold patriarchal mastership she has to deal with. As a result, she carefully formulates her every word and sentence. Knowing well her powerless state, she tries to forward her own claims in the name of all kinds of authorities, religious or secular. She never forgets the modifier "dutiful" whenever she signs her name. Neither will she overlook a chance to name "God" in defense of herself. "On God all future good depends," Pamela once declares in her verses (90). As the source of her courage, the final justification of her action, and her "only refuge" (107), God is at the core of all her words. By bringing "God Almighty" into the talk, she not only voices her righteous intention to reproach Mr. B, but also signals her subtle hope in persuading and converting the young rake. Another "authority" she frequently appeals to is the medieval code of the chivalrous protection of the "fair sex" and the feudal lord's responsibility toward his vassal. Not for nothing does she repeatedly describe herself as "little," "poor," and "worthless." Indeed, Pamela respects very much Mr. B's position as the master and the aristocratic landowner. When expressing her annoyance that "a master of his honour's degree demeans himself to be so free . . . to such a poor servant as me" (29), she sounds more upset about Mr. B's breach of the proper manner of an honorable master/protector than about the actual insult to herself.

Pamela also shows strong Puritan characteristics,[6] especially a firm faith in individual conscience. In the above passage quoted earlier, we see how she—notably, with two lengthy adjective clauses—deduces human worth from the authority of God and shifts the rhetorical emphasis to the individual: "in whose [God's] presence we all stand, in every action of our lives, and to whom the greatest as well as the least, must be accountable. . . ." In the clauses, God is grammatically removed to the place of an object or an attribute, whereas "we" human beings become the subject and the conversational focus. At the same time, an idea of spiritual equality is steadily expressed. Pamela's speeches are marked by her high-pitched moral seriousness and purposefulness: she sentimentally envisions herself as the persecuted "poor maiden" fighting for all the sacred things—the belief in God, the social and moral order, and the dignity and the worth of individual life.

Mr. B, on the contrary, is in a sense speaking for speaking's sake. He is, characteristically, playful, lighthearted, and very creative. He could teasingly imagine Pamela in the clergymen's gown for a moment, and then in a house of prostitution, and enjoys both fictional situations immensely. His rude jokes can hardly help him in any practical sense, not even in his "ambition" to seduce a young girl. He seems to be wholly absorbed in appreciating his own high-spirited and witty blasphemy. If Pamela is paradoxically a staunch defender of order and authority, Mr. B is scandalously sacrilegious toward everything: religion and clergymen; politics and "we parliament members"; the friendship between pious women; the female penchant for romantic writings; the body and honor of the woman to whom he is attracted.

This does not mean that Mr. B is in any way more original or "revolutionary" in attitudes or outlooks. He is almost a stereotype taken directly out of a Restoration comedy, and his cynicism and hedonism are very much a literary, as well as a social, convention. In the worlds of Mr. B/Lovelace, a cynical tongue and the ingenious seduction of a reluctant beauty are valued as much as chastity is in Pamela's circle. His free use of profanity is the stock response of a dissolving social group that no longer believes in any glorifying myth about themselves. The charm and strength of his discourse lie in this very quality of disbelief. Until his acceptance of Pamela's self-mystification, he is rather "realistic" and honest about his own intentions and the obnoxious truth of the existing class and sexual arrangements. Though he misreads Pamela as a little lustful hypocrite, like a Lady Wishfort,[7] he in many ways divines her true mind. When Pamela blushes over his bestowal of some of his late mother's stockings, he smiles: "Don't blush, Pamela: Dost think I don't know pretty maids should wear shoes and stockings?" (12) This measured ironic response shows perhaps the best side of Mr. B as a shrewd speaker. He is amused by the sexual agitation beneath a young girl's "bashfulness" and sneers at the fundamentally hypocritical nature of decorum and propriety. In his words there is always a kind of deconstructive pleasure, which sometimes almost amounts to courage and truthfulness. It is not only as a representative rake, but also as an embodiment of historically recurring disbelief and demystification, that Mr. B has sustained his debate against Pamela's genteel and moralistic voice.[8]

The other fairy tale motif—the contrast and conflict between the kind godmother and the evil stepmother—is also orchestrated and subsumed into the central Pamela/Mr. B confrontation. The mother-like senior servant Mrs. Jervis is a rather ineffective protector and a faint echo of Pamela, but the "wicked" Mrs. Jewkes, whose name and social situation bear a striking resemblance to the other older woman, is on the contrary eloquent, active, and powerful. During Mr. B's absence she not only acts in his interests as a turnkey, a spy, and a bawd, but also speaks on his behalf and carries on the dialogue with Pamela for him. She argues with a sound logic and a down-to-earth realism not very different from that of Mr. B the seducer: "Are not the two sexes made for one another?" (111) Or sometimes she coldly sneers at the girl, sounding almost like an ironical wit: "Mightily miserable, indeed, to be so well beloved by one of the finest gentlemen in England" (112). Mrs. Jewkes is ugly and heavy, physically unfeminine looking, and more importantly, "has a hoarse, *man-like voice*" (116, my emphasis).

The textual tensions of the novel, however, do not begin or end with Pamela's contention with Mr. B; they go much deeper than the surface opposition and negotiation between the protagonists. Self-perceived as the true Christian hero resisting the Satanic tempter, Pamela forcefully denies in herself any worldly ambition or longing for material fulfillment: "For what indeed is happiness,/ But conscience innocence and peace?" (89)

Yet her text, with its disruptive lacunas, discrepancies, and ambiguities, tells a different story. This demure maid persuasively reasons about the necessity of her resistance to Mr. B:

if I was wicked enough, he would keep me till I was undone, and till his mind changed; for even wicked men, I have read, soon grow weary of wickedness with the same person, and love variety. Well, then, poor Pamela must be turned off, and looked upon as a vile abandoned creature, and everybody would despise her; ay, and *justly* too, . . . for she that can't keep her virtue ought to live in disgrace. (36)

What is striking about this speech is not her righteous disdain for the "fallen woman," but her very pragmatic rationale, which could be reduced to a rather utilitarian formula: being "wicked" does not pay in the end. Although we may wonder whether this sophistication is convincing psychologically for a girl of fifteen who has lived a relatively sheltered life up to the moment, it does illuminate an important aspect of this character—she is neither very "innocent," nor very otherworldly. Her insistence on virtue comes at least as much from her concern for her well-being in this world as from her pietism. Given the existing gender arrangement, what can better protect and promote her interest than being justly and laudably conformist? After all, she is by no means as "romantic" about virtue and faith as Mr. B sometimes presumes. We have noticed how she deftly wields the code of conventional goodness, in her prolonged emotional fencing with Mr. B, to retort and argue, to coax and persuade. The gap between the code of modesty and its actual function as a defensive as well as an offensive weapon hints at the covert yet energetic self-assertive impulse on the part of the female paragon.

Such textual discords and discrepancies are part of a programmed pattern, rather than linguistic accidents. The personal desires of the chaste heroine, usually conscientiously suppressed in the text, spring up through these narrative holes and gaps. After Pamela discovers Mr. B's "wickedness," she repeatedly begs for permission to return to her parents. Yet, once the matter is decided, she tarries at his house under the pretense of "the duties" of her place (34). Then, with doubled care and diligence, she makes her best piece of embroidery work—a waistcoat for that "vile" master of hers (35, 39). More intriguingly, she throws herself in the way of Mr. B so often that even her amorous libertine master, who seems at the moment halfheartedly inclined to be done with this little "witch," is more vexed than flattered (34). For all her declared abhorrence of Mr. B's sexual interest in her, Pamela is curiously anxious about his feeling toward her (34, 254). She measures out the exact amount of coy resistance needed to prevent Mr. B from totally losing his appetite. For example, while she is adamant in refusing to be a kept mistress, she takes good care to announce firmly that she loves no one else: "the only one I could honour more than another, is the gentleman, who, of all others, seeks my everlasting dishonour" (198). Tellingly, this announcement is recorded in a straightforward way; no irony or distanced reflections on it are registered in the text. Neither Pamela nor Richardson, the middle-class moral mentor, seems to be embarrassed by the obvious logical and moral incongruity in her honoring the man who wants to "dishonor" her. For them the paradox is natural and necessary. When Mr. B, guided by her doubly oriented utterances and gestures, finally reaches an "honorable" proposal, exultant Pamela even allows herself to pronounce the dangerous word "love" and mentions the existence of her "treacherous, treacherous heart" (260–261). Those ambiguous verbal and behavioral signals, generally in conflict with the heroine's overt moral concerns, clearly denote her desires—her sexual attraction to her young master and her unspeakable "designs" upon him, whether inchoate or relatively self-conscious. Her self-congratulating report of the financial settlement that Mr. B makes on her and her family upon their marriage and her vulgar enthusiasm about playing a "lady" further bear out the fact that this "angel" woman by no means cares only for her deserved spiritual reward "at a time when millions of gold will not purchase one happy moment" (198). Though Pamela never lets herself say "I wish," as Cinderella once does, she nevertheless cautiously navigates her little ship of life to the same harbor of the much desired happy marriage and reaps every prize imaginable, both spiritual and material. Richardson's book might as well be subtitled "Disciplined Desire Rewarded," instead of "Virtue Rewarded."

Therefore, we can see that parallel to Pamela's self-advertised Christian program of trial and salvation, there is the "silent" plot of self-advancement and self-fulfillment, which, though

only suggested by narrative incongruities and ruptures, is finally supported by the overall plot scheme. Peter Brooks defines "plot" as "the organizing line and the intention of
narrative" (37). In this sense, the wish-fulfilling development
of Cinderellean ascent, which is the skeleton, the "organizing
line" of the novel, carries the true "moral" of *Pamela*.

Through the image of marriage, the two plots—the divine one
and the worldly one—are happily welded together. William and
Malleville Haller's study, "The Puritan Art of Love," shows that
even before Milton hailed "wedded love" in *Paradise Lost* (4.750),
the British Puritans already had an energetic literature idealizing
and celebrating marriage. Richardson is very much in line with
this tradition when he presents the married family as the castle of
order, goodness, and harmony. Wedded love, associated with
Eden in Christian myth, is envisaged as an earthly paradise. With
the transfiguration of marriage into a kind of divine reward, the
two plots merge into one. Needless to say, this sacred marriage
as a trope is rich and ambiguous. It half-conceals and half-reveals
the heroine's individualistic desires, since on the one hand the
concept is itself freighted with religious connotations, yet on the
other hand it inescapably points to the sublunary social, financial,
and emotional transactions a marriage actually involves.

Fielding was quick in recognizing the unspoken "asides" of
desire in *Pamela*. His Shamela is consistently self-seeking: "I
thought once of making a little fortune by my Person, I now
intend to make a great one by my Vartue" (53). His parody is
shrewd and entertaining, but not very original. Having de-
ployed in Mr. B a cynical voice against Pamela, Richardson not
only anticipates but in a way forestalls such an interpretation.
Shamela, the boldfaced and consciously snaring hypocrite, indicates a deliberate blindness on Fielding's part to the textual tension between the various voices and inclinations that inhabit
Pamela and *Pamela*. Understandably, the little class-climber
Pamela, with her inner complexity, is not to be deflated easily.
In spite of Fielding's burlesque, this middle-class cinder girl
lives to be a most successful heroine, and the fact that she has so
many literary progeny proves her vitality. With its structuring

image of "war," with its curious and continuous dialogue between the apparently self-effacing protagonist and the wish-fulfilling narrative design, and between the prevailing moralistic discourse of modesty and the individualistic desire that propels it, Richardson's text establishes the paradigm in the English novel for the later flourishing Cinderella theme. This kind of doubleness, self-generating, multileveled and multidimensioned—the double plot, double debate, and doubly oriented language—forms a dynamic "internal dialogism" (Bakhtin 279), and pulses the narrative onward. Here we are not chiefly concerned with the universal dialogic nature of all novelistic language, though I basically agree with Bakhtin on that point. What I want to highlight is the importance of the textual dialectics within the Pamela/Cinderella pattern, which enable and energize a powerful female novelistic tradition.

The thematic and stylistic tension and contention we have noted in *Pamela* are neither isolated nor fortuitous. Lovelace once compares his private "warfare" with Clarissa—which is, he says, "far, far from an amorous warfare"—to the most far-reaching civil war in English history: "if I *must* be forsworn whether I answer her expectations or follow my own inclinations (as Cromwell said, if it must be my head, or the king's) . . . can I hesitate a moment which to choose?" (401–402). The connection is made, though it is somewhat blurred by Lovelace's playfulness and hyperbole. The battle between Clarissa's "expectations" and her pursuer's "inclinations," which is—like the one between Pamela and Mr. B—the wrangle of different literary discourses and plots, is here brought into contact with the social and political history of their nation.

With Richardson, the issues of writing are always intricately entangled with issues outside the text—the problems of gender, manners, morality, and class struggle. When Mr. B first makes his sexual advance toward Pamela, he speaks at the same time of making "a pretty story in Romance" (26). In the farcical scene of his attempted rape, Pamela gives Mrs. Jewkes a formal account of her "history in brief" (211), which half-disarms the listening Mr. B even before her timely fainting fully frustrates him. Mr. B threatens to strip the girl to get her "papers" (245). And, significantly, his final transformation from an evil seducer into a Prince Charming is triggered, as it is described, by Pamela's writings (248–253). In Richardson's world there is an amazing slippage between the "word" and the empirical "life." The paragons guard their writings as vigilantly as their persons, and the profligates who aim at sexual conquest take as much pain to steal, intercept, or read their "words." It is not the fairies, but the right "words" that have the magic power to transform "life" dynamically. When Pamela, expressing her unwillingness to surrender some of her journals, says, "all they contain, *you* know as well as *I*," Mr. B answers: "But I don't know *the light you put things in*" (250–251, my emphasis). What happens next is that the gentleman is overwhelmed by her "light," and reforms into a decent lover.

Passages like these may be taken as self-referential interpretive hints for reading the novel. They seem to be suggesting that there is something beneath or behind the surface story of Pamela's journal letters—the electrifying spiritual "light," the "greater semiological system" (Barthes 116) that can be named "myth"—something of the energy not only to stipulate the life of the fictional characters, but to throw a nation into war. As one of the generation of the mighty moralists who tried hard to remodel English society with their pens and eventually succeeded in replacing the aristocratic fop with the sober and modest Sir Charles Grandisons and Lady Pamelas, Richardson, instead of hiding his didactic purpose, deliberately underscores it and the extraliterary context of his literary creations. This marked intentionality makes his Pamela a telling sample of a powerful social myth of the time, which might be best termed the "Cinderella myth." Mythic Cinderella largely overlaps with the ideal woman figure of "the proper lady": both embrace a social ambition as well as a set of behavioral codes. By naming her "Cinderella," however, I give the myth a slightly different emphasis here: instead of stressing the ideal image and the woman's necessary ethical perfection, her practical plan of class climbing and romantic love is foregrounded.

The fascination with the Cinderella type occurred at the point in time when the "woman problem" had become one of the foremost topics in private and public discussions. From Defoe's ambivalent presentation of the aggressive and unscrupulous Moll and Roxana, or from the self-indulgent amorous heroines populating the semipornographic novels of Mrs. Manley and Eliza Haywood, it may be inferred that there was by then a kind of widespread moral dizziness over the norm of female behavior. In that age of adventure and new possibilities, industrialization and colonization, had fundamentally corroded the old hierarchy and old morality. As middle-class women were phased out of the economic fields, they found themselves thrown into a dazzling yet precarious leisure by the unprecedented wealth created by increasingly specialized means of production. A large quantity of conduct books were eagerly produced and consumed in eighteenth-century England. They are at once a remedy for, and a sure indication of, the existing moral anarchy. All the best pens of England spared no time or energy on this problem: female behavior was no trifling matter for the new bourgeois order. "The Chastity of Women," said Dr. Johnson, very candid about the patriarchal nature of the shaping female code, is "of the utmost importance, as all the property depends upon it" (Boswell 2: 457).

There soon appeared a great mass of propaganda designed to create and promote the new "lady," which was attributed by Defoe to the social ambition of middle-class men: "The tradesman is foolishly vain of making his wife a gentlewoman, forsooth, he will have her sit above in the parlour, receive visits, drink Tea, and entertain her neighbours, or take a coach and go abroad . . ." (*English Tradesman* 1: 292).

By the time Pamela came into being, the ideal image of the new ladylike woman had nearly crystallized. Talking of her unfitness for poor, rural life, Pamela gives a detailed list of her "accomplishments" in singing, dancing, drawing, etc., which, according to Utter and Needham, "covers exactly the items of a lady's education at the time" (10). These skills, together with her unswerving virtue, delicate physique, and maudlin sensibility, are hallmarks of a true lady. In a later book—Frances Burney's *The Wanderer* (1814)—people accept, to different degrees, the "Incognito" as a gentlewoman, basically because of her musical talents and her educated way of speaking. Properly cultivated and publicly recognizable ladylike women were among the first luxuries that the newly rich could boast of. Woman was as much a circulating "signifier" in the transactions among men as she had been for the Restoration rakes, though she was inserted into the scenario of a different social drama.

By this I mean not just to reassert, as many feminist critics have already eloquently demonstrated,[9] the patriarchal bias of the Cinderella dream, but to call attention to the fact that on the ideological spectrum, the dream to a considerable degree overlaps with more overtly male-concerned and male-centered conceptions like "gentleman." The lady is the gentlewoman, just as Cinderella has her more realistic male counterpart in the legendary hard-working apprentice who eventually marries his master's daughter and comes into the ownership of the business.[10] They are the complementary facets of the same cultural myth, and therefore in many ways share the same kind of inner dichotomy and dialectics.

A deafening chorus in praise of the Protestant virtues of modesty, restraint, self-denial, and absolute chastity accompanied the emergence of the new middle-class gentleman and lady. The most striking thing about this moral-linguistic hubbub is its immanent self-contradictions. Sacvan Bercovitch, in *The Puritan Origins of the American Self,* explores this "paradox of Christic identity, with its double focus on fact and ideal, activism and self-denial":

Modern historians of the Reformation claim that "self from now on stands for man," as though this meant an increased sense of personal worth. The Puritan's understanding of that phrase begins with Augustine: "Two loves have given origin to these two cities, self-love in contempt of God . . . [and] love of God in contempt of one's self. . . . ." As the Puritans

developed and amplified the conflict, self-versus-God became
the motivating force of their activism. . . . (17)

He continues: "The basis of Puritan psychology lies in this contrast between personal responsibility and individualism. We can
say, with William Haller, that they believed 'man's chief concern should be with the welfare of his own soul' " (16–17).

Leopold Damrosch, too, has in similar terms discussed this
self-conflicting nature of "Puritan individualism," which he
calls "the paradoxical union of self-analysis and self-denial" (4).
In addition, the split between the content of these writings—
the teaching of humbleness, restraint, and quietude—and their
ardent, pushing, sometimes neurotic, sometimes overbearing
style forcefully tells of this paradox. As Bercovitch states, after
an examination of writings of a number of Puritan spokesmen,
the very style in which they put forward the necessity for a
severe policing of the self—"the vehemence of the metaphors,
the obsessiveness of the theme, the staccato syntax, . . . the
interminable-because-unresolved incantations of the 'I' over
itself'—"betrays a consuming involvement with 'me' and
'mine'" (18). In other words, Puritan virtue is not envisioned
as a static quality, but a process, a constant struggle. By posit-
ing the self as the archenemy, the Devil or Antichrist (Bercovitch 18), the Puritan heightened the importance of the individual in a paradoxical, or negative, way.

This does not imply, however, that such ascetic Protestantism serves its upholder's self-interest only in a negative way.
The clamorous chant over virtue was almost a war cry. In its
very conception, Puritan goodness not only presupposes an inward enemy, the self, but also an outward one. The code of
modesty itself was a "challenge" to prevailing upper-class manners (Gilmour 10). This polemical position has clear expressions
in the fictional works that consciously advocate virtue, in which
the upper-class villain is the indispensable foil and interlocutor
of the pious protagonists.[11] It is to this Satanic enemy-debater
of mythical stature that the "quiet," "unassuming" middle-
class lady/gentleman owes her/his heroic role as a moral and
cultural crusader.

Equally revealing of the aggressive aspect of the code of modesty is its open and secure "marriage" to worldly success. Max Weber has demonstrated how the Protestant spirit of self-restraint is most necessary and helpful for the capitalistic "pursuit of profit, and forever renewed profit" (17). Lady Pamela and Sir Charles Grandison personify goodness, but at the same time they mark a relatively prestigious status aspired to by the eighteenth-century bourgeoisie. The title "gentleman" or "lady" itself implies property, leisure, and style. Pamela's "accomplishments" are important exactly because they are skills of no practical use and therefore become a sign of the freedom from poverty and manual labor and a visa to the moneyed and leisured social group. For Pamela, social advancement and material gains are so naturally wedded to virtue that she is unashamedly snobbish once her chance appears secure. The same kind of snobbishness can also be discerned in Elizabeth Bennet or Fanny Price, Cinderellas who are yet unscathed by any serious criticism within Austen's novels. With the deferred happy ending that crowns good speaking and good deed, the practice of virtue becomes a wish-fulfilling program.[12]

In this light we can neither denounce the code of propriety and the ascetic Protestantism underpinning it as merely, or primarily, sexist, oppressive, and debilitating from the twentieth-century feminist point of view; nor can we overhastily claim, as critics like Mary Poovey or Gilbert and Gubar suggest, that female desire (which may be under various names, such as "will," "appetite," "selfhood," "self-assertion," and so on), and especially women's spontaneous, sexual desire, is by nature opposed or subversive to the patriarchy and the bourgeois order as a whole.[13] The very concept of "desire" as we understand it—as the natural impulse for self-fulfillment, the romantic "monster," and the repressed "id" inherently in conflict with the demands of the society—is quintessentially Western and bourgeois. The desire/self-denial pair is in a sense a "false" opposition, since both are legitimately placed within the dialectics of modern individualism. Each age may have its own accent, but the ideological dialectic between the poles has been going on for several hundred years.[14] Many feminists have justly argued about the victimization of women through ideological apparatuses like moral codes and cultural myths. Yet, at the same time, we should pay greater attention to the larger cultural framework, to which the above-discussed ideological and textual dialogues belong. George Levine in *The Realistic Imagination* notices that the "passive hero" impersonating modesty and self-restraint is typical of all "realistic" novels. In a lengthy note to Chapter Two he points out the parallel between his study and *The Madwoman in the Attic.* "Yet," he then continues, "my argument is that the 'monstrous' is an aspect of *all* realistic literature, that the repression of it is part of the strategy of realism, not exclusively or even primarily of women's literature. Interestingly, Bersani, calling the monster 'desire,' detects the same pattern" (331).

This dichotomy between self-denial and self-fulfillment, in various forms and expressions, underlies most English bourgeois moral ideals. When I say that *Pamela* has reshaped "Cinderella" into a modern myth, I mean not only that Pamela, as the finally victorious cinder girl, is naturally the embodiment of the social ambitions of the middle-class would-be ladies, but more emphatically that the novel ingeniously grafts the central dialectics of Protestant individualism onto the structural ambiguity of the original tale.

Thus we come to a basic assumption of the present study—the fundamentally dialectic nature of Puritan ethics and of ideology in general. On this point I differ from Bakhtin considerably. Bakhtin, though stressing the "inner dialogism" of all words and languages in a general way, claims that authoritative discourse "is by its very nature incapable of being double voiced; it cannot enter into hybrid constructions" (344).[15] As I perceive it, ideology, being a class consciousness, is necessarily polemic and posed against other ideologies; and, as a living and effectively functioning language system, it must constantly receive feedback and be under continuous construction. Even the ideology of the ruling group, that is, "the authoritative discourse" in the social and cultural spheres, can only strive to unify and monopolize language; but it can never achieve this end, else it would wipe itself out. The energetic efforts to censor *words,* as Richardson did with his own text, testify to, instead of clear away, the recognized heteroglot quality of the discourse. "Ideology always contains contradictions," Mary Poovey argues, "precisely because it 'explains' or 'naturalizes' the discrepancies that inevitably characterize lived experience" (xiv).

All social strata and/or classes build their ideological apparatus with inherited linguistic materials; therefore, in a sense all the words and concepts adopted by the "new" system are inevitably "kidnapped" and "violated." There is, then, an ongoing friction and negotiation between the inert and more crystallized linguistic form and the new emphasis and new intention imposed on it. Such a self-conflicting system is the whole set of Puritan ideas about sin, virtue, and salvation, with all the semantic sediment accumulated since Old Testament time. So are the conceptions of the "lady" and "gentleman." Drawing on both their medieval roots and the new middle-class moral concern, the signifying process of these terms is a kind of oscillation between different poles, or perhaps more accurately, a dancing around through various aspects and layers of the "signified." This ambiguity is self-consciously exploited by the middle-class people who cash in on their moral goodness. When Elizabeth Bennet says: "He [Darcy] is a gentleman; I am a gentleman's daughter, so far we are equal" (366), she is carefully playing on both the social and moral implications of the term "gentleman." Neither will it need extraordinary acumen to realize how Puritanism is intercepted and permeated by other ideas, say, the Benthamite rational affirmation of the pursuit of personal happiness, or the Lockean empirical emphasis on subjective sensations. The Cinderella tale as an equivocal and promising narrative pattern provides an ideal meeting ground where different modes of philosophical and ideological thinking can confront, negotiate, and merge with each other. Pamela's ready tears and Emmeline's cool calculations indicate more than their personal idiosyncrasies. These Lady-Cinderellas are ideological compounds and register the intrinsic compatibility as well as the contradictions of these value systems.

In a word, Puritanism as a local version of the newly emerging individualism is "impure" and self-contradictory. Its clamorous cry of self-denial is the inseparable other face of bourgeois ideology, since ideology as centripetal group consciousness must by definition be collective, idealistic, and "utopian" (Jameson 289). The idealistic enthusiasm and moral discipline that such ascetic Protestantism brought about were especially needed for the post-Renaissance middle class, which had yet to fight for its footing in all social, economic, and cultural arenas. The Puritan formula of self-denial seeks both to convey and to disguise individualism, both to promote it and to contain it. Bourgeois ideology, as well as the related myths, are especially paradoxical and protean because of this individualistic core, which cannot but run counter to the collective and "utopian" nature of ideology itself.

As a result, the Cinderella myth has functioned as a double-edged (or multiedged) ideological weapon. On the one hand, the code of propriety is carefully woven into a myth that romanticizes woman's subordinate and domesticated role within the patriarchy; on the other hand, the Protestant individualism that is simultaneously programmed into the plot inevitably arouses in women (and underprivileged people in general) a sense of individual dignity and an urge for self-realization. We hear Clarissa insist on her "freedom," which is her "birthright as an English Subject" (934). We also witness how those proper ladies, fictional Pamelas or "real" Frances Burneys, exhibit a profound interest in themselves and a remarkable faith in the meaningfulness of their private lives. Such self-consciousness, once it begins to ferment, can hardly be safely imprisoned in the narrow space of a bourgeois marriage. Even Pamela, the model wife, sometimes sounds dangerous. When her husband gives her a long list of rules to follow and specifically demands her obedience to his unreasonable orders, she says to herself, "this would bear a smart debate, I fancy, in a Parliament of Women" (477). A Parliament of Women! Truly, there is no saying what can get into women's minds once they are set to thinking and "fancying" by Richardsonian ideologues. It is not surprising that they would push the principles they have been taught one step further, as Mary Wollstonecraft does from the Right of Man to the Right of Woman.

In this sense the Cinderella myth is self-defeating as far as its patriarchal purpose is concerned. The kind of individualism it conveys is too energetic and aggressive to be contained by the ideological closure in which the happy marriage symbolizes a reestablished patriarchal order.

This can perhaps account for the obscurity that the Cinderella tale drifted into in the old Chinese literature. Many Chinese folk tales, especially the great four I mentioned in the Preface ("Madame White Snake," "Meng Jiang," "The Story of the Shepherd Boy and the Weaving Girl," and "Liang Shan-bo and Zhu Ying-tai") are still vital, living traditions, familiar to people rich and poor, old and young, through oral storytelling and popular theatrical performances. They also find frequent expressions in folk songs, various local customs, or even in "highbrow" classical poetry.[16] Yet, for nearly a thousand years the story of Cinderella simply did not penetrate into the Chinese mainstream Han culture. Its "disappearance" seems so complete that, as far as I know, not even any considerable conscious attempt to repress or distort the story has been discovered. It was not until modern Western countries opened China's "door" with warships that the Chinese imported (or perhaps more accurately, reimported), among many other things, the Cinderella tale. Within a very oppressive and stratified society, where no social mobility was imaginable on the part of a woman, and no inspiring individualism was allowed, the tale simply lost its magic and fell into a kind of cultural oblivion.

In the following chapters, I will discuss the transformation of the Cinderella theme in a group of novels by several women writers. The focus on women is not arbitrary. It is well known that the story of Pamela's Cinderellean adventure was originally "concocted" by Richardson for women, with an eye to teach them to live and write properly—hence the conscientious "dutiful" protagonist and the wonderful turn in fortune realized exclusively through love and marriage. Both these features accorded with the narrow domestic and domesticated role assigned to women by the shaping middle-class culture. In

Richardson's time, even those who cared about a woman's education and welfare unconsciously regarded her merely as useful living object. When Defoe proposes to establish "an academy for women," he argues: "What Care do we take to Breed up a good Horse, and to Break him well! and what a Value do we put upon him when it is done, and all because he shou'd be fit *for our use! and why not a Woman?*" ("An Academy" 35, my emphasis). The comparison between the draught animal and a woman is extremely revealing about the woman's place in her male master's eye. For all the education, all the dignified spirituality those liberal men may bestow on women, the precious gender hierarchy is not to be disturbed. Richardson, the male precursor who introduced Cinderella into the English novel, was very cautious about the possible subversive implications of Pamela's battle against her master. When he gives all kind of social advice to his female audience through the practical "injunctions" Pamela receives from her husband, we cannot help but realize that he, too, aims at making woman "suitable and serviceable" (Defoe, "An Academy" 35).

Small wonder that the Cinderella myth as Richardson reformulates it does not quite suit the middle-class male figure in the English novel, who, as an active businessman, entrepreneur, or professional, is expected to make a profit, to succeed, and to conquer. Men may share Cinderella's social aspirations, but, when they happen to think in terms of this archetype, they have to combine it with other more aggressive male models. David Copperfield is obliged to add successful professional work to the help he receives from his eccentric aunt, a recognizable fairy figure; young Pip, while dreaming of a godmother to transform him magically, understands that in order to marry the "Princess," he has to "do all the shining deeds of the young knight of romance" (Dickens, *Great Expectations* 253).[17]

It is true that male writers after Richardson often based their heroines on the Cinderella type. We can classify, with certain qualifications, Dickens's Esther or Lizzie Hexam in this group; and little Jenny Wren, crippled and poor, is named in the narrative as "Cinderella" (Dickens, *Our Mutual Friend* 492, 796)— perhaps with some intentional irony, since no Prince Charming is ever interested in the very poor and maimed like her. Thackeray, on the other hand, bitterly satirizes Richardson's Pamela by naming Becky Sharp's little booth in Vanity Fair "Virtue Rewarded."

It is, however, in the hands of women writers that the narrative pattern prospers and gains emotional and existential urgency. I have already mentioned how the fictional works by women writers are crowded with cinder girls—for more than a century after *Pamela,* the Cinderellean happy ending is still the only victory and happiness imaginable for most women. It is their lot to live, and to struggle, with this romantic dream. Of the hundreds of Cinderella narratives, the present study will focus on four major novels by Frances Burney, Charlotte Smith, Jane Austen, and Charlotte Brontë. Young ladies like Belinda, to be sure, are as well qualified as any of the heroines more closely examined here. However, this is not meant to be an exhaustive study of all works patterned on the Cinderella plot. Rather, the individual novels discussed here are to be taken as synecdochal in illustrating the various ways in which women writers have responded and reacted to this male-initiated literary convention.

I propose to read these novels as, to borrow Terry Castle's words, "a congeries, a cluster of disparate discourses" (27), and to approach them through a close examination of the dialogue and the interaction between the clashing and mediating discourses, styles, and plot schemes. Such textual dialogue is necessarily multidimensioned and multilayered. As I have maintained, the Cinderella theme is itself essentially ambiguous and dialogic, with a constant tension built on the desire/self-denial, passion/reason dichotomy. The women writers who immediately followed in Richardson's footsteps seemed to have understood the nature of such ideological dialectic better than some modern critics. Instead of absolutizing the opposition between the two sides, they instinctively grasped its individualistic essence. Their novels show how the ideal Cinderella plunges deep into this discursive dialogue and successfully conducts it to a self-asserting end. Legions of heroines like Evelina, Cecilia, or Belinda, conjured up by literary women, testify to the libidinal energy with which women embraced this double role represented by Cinderella—the romantic beloved and the moral guard of their class.

No less importantly, an implied negotiation is also being carried out between the female authors and the established narrative pattern itself. There is a natural ambivalence on the part of the women writers. The formulaic plot confines woman in a secondary, dependent, and carefully defined "feminine" role, even though it at the same time allows a meaning for individual life that seems to transcend gender and class differences and leaves a limited "free" space where female subjectivity is able to sprout and grow. As the marginalized sex that is "both of the culture and out of it (or under it)" (Miller 38), women could not but uncomfortably sense the alien, even hostile patriarchal mentality embedded in the narrative. Generations of women novelists seemed to be troubled by their problematic position within this male-initiated and male-formulated tradition, and their works display a hypersensitivity in this regard. Consciously or unconsciously, they endeavor to feminize the convention through all kinds of narrative tactics and strategies—twisting the plot and adding their own emphasis (Miller 38); playing the game of "double talk," "evasion," and "concealment"; deploying an underground second plot (Gilbert and Gubar 49, 74–75). Just as Pamela dexterously manipulates the socially ratified discourses to serve herself, women novelists intuitively develop the paradox of the existing Cinderella theme, explore it from a feminine or feminist angle, and stretch it to create a larger imaginative, as well as existential, space. Austen manages to reflect on the narrative tradition by tackling Fanny Price's tricky inarticulateness; in *Villette,* Brontë presents a spectating outsider as the heroine and thereby drastically rewrites the character type. Trying to tailor their female experience and sensibility to the inherited narrative paradigm, they end up by retailoring the paradigm itself and parading their Otherness. And it is this entangled verbal wrestling that gives the texts by women their special power and vitality.

The multiplicity of the woman's language in every way further complicates the textual dialogue within these novels. This female linguistic multiplicity is not just a mechanical mirroring of the dialogism and cacophony of the dominant language of Protestant individualism that is marketed to women in a wholesale way by the male authority. It is more the result of the diversity and disparity of female lives and female attitudes—there is no abstractly unified Woman with a capital *W,* but many concrete women of different family, class, racial, and national backgrounds. Lauretis talks affirmatively about "women's heterogeneous subjectivity and multiple identity" "engendered across multiple representations of class, race, language, and social relations" (14). Novels are fictional expressions of this multiplicity of female experience. If Wollstonecraft's sentimental Maria represents a frustrated romantic love, her "hard-boiled" lower-class Jemima's struggle through various employments certainly suggests some different concerns. If Burney's Evelina and Juliet are conceived as paragon ladies, then her "odd" women—Mrs. Selwyn and Elinor Joddrel, with their contrasting sayings and doings—give a new dimension and a new edge to the story of the paradigmatic cinder girl.

In this book I will try to follow this complex textual dialogue in its various dimensions and forms, and to show how Cinderella's narrative pattern is being appropriated, reshaped, and eventually disrupted by these women writers. Since the Cinderella myth is very much an embodiment of a bourgeois ideology in respect to gender arrangement, women's rewriting of the myth can also be read as an index to a growing female self-consciousness, and as a political gesture of a marginal social group toward certain ruling ideas. When Charlotte Brontë finally brushes away the expected wedding from the last page of *Villette,* it is an interesting and significant moment not only in the evolution of the Cinderella theme in the English novel, but also in the growth of a vigorous and potentially mutinous female subjectivity, which, at that point, can no longer be contained by the narrative pattern that has bought it into being.

CHAPTER ONE

Evelina: *"With a Consciousness of Her Sex"*

O Author of my being!—far more dear To me than
  light, than nourishment, or rest,
Hygieia's blessings, Rapture's burning tear Or the
  life blood that mantles in my breast!

. . . .

Could my weak pow'rs thy num'rous virtues trace,
  By filial love each fear should be repress'd;
The blush of incapacity I'd chace,
  And stand, recorder of thy worth, confess'd.
                      —Frances Burney: "Introductory
                        Ode" to *Evelina*

Frances Burney devotedly dedicated *Evelina* (1778) to the
"Authors" of her being: Dr. Burney and/or "Daddy" Crisp.
Her journals show that before revealing her authorship, she
worried greatly about their opinions of the book. Paternal authority is the source of her worry, but it is also somehow
wielded by her to vindicate her presumptuous action of author-
ing a book and ward off possible censure. In her relationship to
these towering fathers, as is shown in this high-flown ode, there
is a fusion and confusion of love and fear. Fear is conveyed by
a warm declaration of love, and an uneasy sense of dependence
is mixed with tender attachment. This verbal and emotional
ambiguity, which is at the core of Burney's personality, also
forms a dynamic tension in the narrative of *Evelina*.

In *Pamela,* the women characters, "good" or "bad," no longer
have any decisive influence upon the outcome of an event. Patriarchal figures have already replaced those female family members that were so important in the fairy tale as the "persecutors."
It is as if "Cinderella" suddenly outgrows the nursery room fre-
quented by a mother and ventures into the wider outside world,

which is ruled by men. However, a heroine like Pamela, as envisioned by a man, is still able to enjoy a relatively secure relationship with her male spiritual authorities. "I am prepared for the worst," Pamela writes to her father, "for though I fear there will be nothing omitted to ruin me, and though my poor strength will not be able to defend me, yet I will be innocent of crime in my intention, and in the sight of God; and to him leave the avenging of all my wrongs, in his own good time and manner" (197). Although she is yet unsure about Mr. B, she is confident of her own incorruptible purity and of her father's approval. She proudly talks about the sixteen years that she has lived "in moral and reputation," and claims that she is persecuted, like a martyr, for "daring to adhere to the good lessons that were taught me" (210). Similarly, Clarissa, certain of her essential goodness, views her death as the union with God.

The picture alters greatly when drawn from a different angle by a female hand. In *Evelina* we witness the "withdrawal" of God. The heroine no longer trusts in, nor cares much about, God's final justice, but instead anxiously courts the support of her worldly "fathers." Like Bunyan's Christiana, Evelina Anville (Belmont) seems unable to hear God unless through some male mediator, and thus clings to *his* judgment. Innocent as she is, she is never sure about how the "world" will take her, since for her the rules concerned with woman's behavior, which are laid down by those powerful males and inscribed with all kinds of arbitrary social conventions and prejudices, are at once uncongenial and baffling. Her fear, unlike Pamela's, is not first and foremost related to the object of heterosexual love; rather, it suggests a very problematic relationship toward the narratively valorized ideal patriarchal order.

Patricia Meyer Spacks shrewdly points out that fear, the "female fear—not of the absence of power but of failure of goodness and consequent loss of love" (158)—is a vital force in all Burney's writings. What I think needs further exposition, which Spacks only touches upon without exploration, is the fascinating complicity between fear and love. Sheer fear, what Evelina feels in the dark paths of Vauxhall, plays a much less important role in Evelina's (or Burney's) psychological activity. A good example is her relationship with Lord Orville, a kind of fear-generating love. Not that she is, like Pamela, in any way uncertain of the character of the beloved man. Rather, it is exactly his faultlessness, his resemblance to the good father figure, that intimidates Evelina. She is free and sprightly when she feels no necessity to love and respect. At the first few balls, she laughs openly in the face of a ludicrously dressed Mr. Lovel. And she truly surprises us when, in addition to telling Sir Clement her displeasure with him in a most bewitchingly candid way, she boldly eyes Lord Orville while at the same time fictionalizing about her nonexistent preengaged partner for a dance. The very contemptibility of the other party seems to liberate and embolden her. "I am very indifferent as to his opinion," declares Evelina in response to the "strange, provoking, and ridiculous conduct" of Sir Clement (43–44). Yet the girl is overwhelmed as soon as she lays eyes on the "perfect" Lord Orville. She immediately agrees, at once excited and scared, to dance with this young stranger, never bothered by the inconsistency of this move. During her dance with Orville, she "was seized with such a panic," that she "could hardly speak a word." Later, as she is being further tormented by her "new alarms" (26), caused by the information that her partner is a nobleman, Lord Orville is casually commenting on her as a *"silent,"* "poor weak girl" (31). The sharp contrast of their first impressions is most illuminating. Each is obviously attracted to the other. Yet Orville is cool and carefree, even with a slight ironical tongue, and for the only time in the book, he speaks lightly and amusingly; whereas Evelina is almost shattered by her dread and is overwhelmed by a consciousness of Orville's utmost importance as a judge as well as a potential husband. Though as ignorant of the rules of social manners as when she is dealing with Lovels and Clements, Evelina, instead of giggling or making excuses nonchalantly, retrogresses into a scared and inarticulate child who "perpetually fear[s] doing something wrong" (26). When Clement Willoughby deliberately uncovers her little lie before Orville, she is totally unsettled by embarrassment, shame, and the fear that Orville might think her "both bold and presuming" (44). This is almost a moment of epiphany in which Evelina undergoes a decisive process of what may be called "self-objectification." Suddenly she intuits a "great truth" of her world, that is, what she feels or likes is of no weight at all; what matters is the opinion of the *others,* of these Orvilles, even Clements—the judgment of the majestic Magic Mirror of the patriarchal order.[1] Duly she has cultivated an alienated view in relation to herself; she begins to see herself through others' eyes and feels more and more uneasy about her natural urges and reactions.

For her father Sir Belmont—whom, she forcefully proclaims she "yearns to know, and longs to love" (344)—Evelina has an intense fear, but no intimate feelings. Scattered throughout the letter describing her fateful first meeting with her father are words like "terror," "fears," "dread," "agitation" and "trembling." "This unhappy affair," "this dreaded meeting," "the wished,—yet terrible moment," as Evelina refers to it beforehand, generates in her "extreme terror" and a "thousand conjectures and apprehensions." She is "almost senseless with fear" during her ride to the meeting, and at the first sight of her father, she sinks to the floor (344–346). Then, after recording Sir Belmont's reluctance to face her, Evelina the storyteller asks: "Oh Sir, had I not indeed cause to *dread* this interview?—an interview so *unspeakably painful and afflicting to us both!*" (346–347, my emphasis). Evelina has intuited the truth of their relationship: for John Belmont she is a living accusation, a token of an unpleasant past, and a threatening fortune hunter from nowhere; whereas for Evelina the father is inseparably connected with desertion, abuse, and the death of her mother. Her panic is thus more related to the tense and confrontational situation than to any filial love. As a tricky, equivocal word, "fear" harbors implicit hostility yet at the same times expresses some sentiment close to respect and tribute.

Nevertheless, Evelina's alleged love for her father is by no means mere affectation. The heroine gives some clue to her feeling when she, refusing to allow Orville to represent her in the coming negotiations with her father, claims: "it would be highly improper I should dispose of myself for ever, so very near the time which must finally decide by whose authority I ought to be guided" (344). At another decisive moment, when

Lord Orville asks her to marry him, she informs him with cha-
grin and sadness that "I hardly know myself to whom I most
belong" (328). Language like this throws light upon the eco-
nomics of her love. Central to her sense of identity as a woman
is the male "master"—the bread provider as well as the moral
guide—the man to whom she "belongs." The psychological
need to be attached to a man is as strong as the social and financial ones. Herein lies the significance of the *father*, even though
he is as blamable as Sir Clement. After all, he is the first man
from whom Evelina feels herself entitled to claim love and protection by her birthright. Furthermore, being highly class conscious, Evelina, the sharp observer of styles and manners and
the heavy-handed satirizer of her "vulgar" tradesmen relations
from her mother's side, must know well the difference between
a baronet's heiress and "a country parson's daughter" (32). It is
clearly understood by Evelina, and all her helpers, that upon
this inadequate father hangs her only hope of acquiring a legitimate name, which is the passport to that prestigious society in
which she would like to live. Hence her anxious desire to for-
give and love; hence her disproportionate fear of a truant father
who is virtually nonexistent for her.

Evelina's relationship to Rev. Mr. Villars—the old guardian
who has brought her up and adores her indulgently—is more
subtle and complicated. The girl is relatively sure of his unfailing support and always regards his house as her last refuge.
However, she gradually senses the pressure of his moral teachings and discerns the latent threat in such kind warnings as
"nothing is so delicate as the reputation of a woman" (152). It
is not just a passing whim that makes her try to hide from old
Villars her unfortunate exchange of letters with, supposedly,
Orville. When the observant old man finds her very depressed
and distracted, he confronts her directly:

> "My child, I can no longer be a silent witness of thy sorrow
> . . . and ought I be a stranger to the cause . . . ?"
> "Cause, Sir!" cried I, greatly alarmed, "what cause?—I
> don't know,—I can't tell—I—"
> "Fear not," said he, kindly, "to unbosom thyself to me,

. . . open to me thy whole heart,—it can have no feelings for which I will not make allowance. . . . "

"You are too good, too good," cried I, greatly embarrassed; "but indeed I know not what you mean." (246)

Tellingly, Evelina feels not much safer with the good father than with the bad one. She evades and pretends and lies, because she instinctively knows that at the moment she cannot afford to lose Villars's love and protection. Not even his benevolent promise of understanding could convince her. As always, it is the sense of insecurity that controls Evelina's love, or more accurately, her desire to be loved: without financial independence, being loved is the best—perhaps the only—insurance policy a girl can obtain. It would be wrong to read Evelina as downright self-interested or pragmatic. Nevertheless, for her, as for her creator Frances Burney and many women of her time, the psychological need for heterosexual affection functions, at least partly, as a strategy for individualistic survival.

For Evelina, the words "fear" and "love" are almost interchangeable. If she often covers her anxiety, caused by old Villars's patriarchal goodness, with effusive proclamations of "love," with Lord Orville the case is sometimes the reverse: she smuggles in "unspeakable," ambitious romantic love in the name of the legitimate "fear." She talks about Orville in terms of a father figure that naturally demands reverence and love. When lamenting her temporary disillusion with Orville, she compares him to Villars: "Once, indeed, I thought there existed another,—who, *when time had wintered o'er his locks,* would have shone forth among his fellow-creatures, with the same brightness of worth which dignifies my honoured Mr. Villars . . ." (243). Orville's resemblance to that exemplary father/mentor seems to be a full justification of her admiration and partiality for him. She is very lavish in proclaiming his merits and is extremely straightforward in propagandizing her "fear" for him.

No one misreads her "fear" in this regard, nor does she intend anyone to. Marriage and wifehood as a girl's only calling are on everyone's mind. Her girlfriend teases her about her love for Orville, whereas worried Villars openly admonishes her. Here her

self-advocated "fear" of Orville should be taken at its face value
and as a verbal tactic. The fear is real and tormenting in the sense
that an insecure cinder girl cannot help but be frightened by a
possible prince/savior. Yet on the other hand, psychologically
and linguistically, "fear" performs a displacement that enables
the girl to communicate with herself and her friends about the
dangerous topic of sexual attraction, or, even more scandalously,
about her repressed sense of alienation from the existing order.
Pamela, as Wolff notices, smugly talks about her "fearfulness"
even before Mr. B makes any definite advance. This unmistakably tells of Pamela's own expectation (Wolff 62) of some romantic entanglement (possibly in the form of abuse and sexual
violation) between Mr. B and herself. Somewhat unlike the case
with Pamela, fear in Evelina does not quite signify an adolescent
ambivalence toward the lustful "monster" man and heterosexual
love itself, but instead suggests a female sense of social and moral
insecurity. However, a respectful fear or a fearful respect does
allow Evelina to deal with her own love plot in an oblique way:

> I think I rather recollect a *dream*, or some *visionary fancy*, than
> a *reality*. That I should ever have been known to Lord
> Orville,—that I should have spoken to—have danced with
> him, seems now a *romantic illusion*: and that elegant polite-
> ness, that flattering attention, that high-bred delicacy, which
> so much distinguished him above all other men, and which
> struck us with such admiration, I now re-trace the remem-
> brance of, rather as belonging to an object of ideal perfection,
> formed by my own *imagination*, than to a being of the same
> race and nature as those with whom I at present converse.
> (159–160, my emphasis)

Being a worthy student of Villars, who warns her repeatedly
against her "imagination," "fancy," and "passion," Evelina
names her involvement with Orville a "romantic illusion." She
has the sense of unreality all along. Even in her first excitement
about London life, she compares the splendid place where she
comes across Orville for the second time to the "inchanted castle, or fairy palace" (33). Her sensible allusions to "dream" and

fairy tale suggest two kinds of fear: one is her awe of such a faultless male paragon; the other is the apprehension that this personified Goodness and his interest in her may after all turn out to be delusive. Although Evelina believes she is trying hard to draw a line between fairy tale fantasy and "realistic" probability, her efforts to distance herself from her own infatuation with Orville betray instead both her fear and her love. From the perspective of her relatively tranquil country life—she may at least be sure of a small income from Villars and "the pleasures of humble retirement"(16)—her self-indulgent fascination with Orville, based on slight acquaintance, is quite an emotional gamble, which is in itself a source of worry. Propelled by a mental as well as physical hunger for a more substantial, colorful life, and a desire for a new "career" under a new male protector, Evelina quietly but nevertheless stubbornly persists in her risky business of loving. She chooses to see in Orville a more acceptable and less frightening kind of authority, as she loudly praises him: "so *feminine* his delicacy, and so amiable his nature!" (244). This tribute, however, is clearly more related to the "ideal perfection" formed by her "imagination" than to the "real" Orville, of whom we, and Evelina as well, know too little to shape any definite idea (our good-looking hero does nothing throughout the story except ask Evelina to dance, conduct a few dull conversations, and finally propose to her).

By highlighting the motif of fear and yoking it to the female love of the ideal, authoritative male, Frances Burney has made a remarkable contribution to the Cinderella narrative. With its dissenting yet mutually interchangeable two sides, the love/fear pair is continuously intercepted by and interpenetrated with the dialogism between self-denial and self-assertion that I discussed in the Introduction. Of course, there is no simple correspondence between them. That is to say, we cannot equate "love" with self-realization and "fear" with self-repression, or the reverse. In Burney, on the surface both love and fear betoken an effort of conformation and self-denial on the part of a woman; yet at the same time, the double-mode mentality is being appropriated to serve her own survival or even her social advancement. The love/fear complex not only bares the hidden social and financial

coercion behind a woman's attachment to her beloved male master—be it a father, a teacher, or a husband—but also reveals how
the ideologically ratified "fear" and respect for the good patriarch are manipulated by women. Spacks's study shows that
throughout her life Frances Burney herself was an authentic and
experienced "fearer" who carefully avoided any "wrong" step
objected to by her male mentors. Yet, ironically, when she was
over forty and decided to marry "poor M. d'Arblay," she stead-
fastly ignored her father's sound and strongly worded advice and
stuck to her romantic attachment. Though sometimes she still
sounds like an adolescent Evelina and timidly solicits her father's
consent; though she still sees herself through others' eyes and
tries conscientiously to pacify the general amazement over her
unexpected late marriage, Burney is firm and mature when she
writes down the following in her diary: "Happiness is the great
end of all our worldly views & proceedings; & no one can judge
for another in what will produce it" (Hemlow 2: 179). Surely a
woman who thinks like this knows what she is doing and is not
easily scared. The image of fearfulness that she creates for herself,
as Evelina does in a more naive, crude way, is to a degree a protection, a cover to shield the vulnerable true self beneath. For
Frances Burney, as well as for Evelina, love/fear toward the respected paternal figures is at once an inescapable existential con-
dition and a useful mask, no matter what they choose to think, or
say, about it.

Another important addition Burney makes to the narrative
pattern of *Pamela*/Cinderella is the theme of "progress," or "education." Some critics are reluctant to count *Evelina* a *Bildungsroman*, since the protagonist seems to be a static figure
(Adelstein 38). It is true that all Burney's heroines are morally
"completed" before their "first appearance upon the great and
busy stage of life" (Burney, *Evelina* xiii). As the author summarizes it in her preface to the book, when Evelina is ushered onto
the scene, she is already armed "with a virtuous mind, a cultivated understanding, and a feeling heart." The only possible
progress she can make is to overcome her "ignorance of the

forms, and inexperience in the manners, of the world" (xiii). What seems to have escaped the notice of these commentators, however, is the striking shift of style in Evelina's writing, which indicates that the knowledge of the "forms" and "manners" is not a superficial acquirement, but has far-reaching effects upon a young woman's conception of her personality and social role.

When we first hear her, Evelina sounds exactly like a naive country girl dazzled by the enigmatic and colorful city life. Her praise of Mr. Garrick's theatrical performance is extravagant and rapturous:

> Such ease! such vivacity in his manner! such grace in his motions! such fire and meaning in his eyes! . . .
>
> His action—at once so graceful and so free!—his voice—so clear, so melodious, yet so wonderfully various in its tones—such animation!—every look *speaks*!
>
> I would have given the world to have had the whole play acted over again. And when he danced—O how I envied Clarinda! I almost wished to have jumped on the stage and joined them. (22)

However understandable the youthful enthusiasm conveyed by this long string of exclamation marks, it is definitely "un-lady-like" to get so overly and overtly excited about a play. Virginia Woolf wonderfully recaptures this breathless, girlish style in "Fanny Burney's Half-Sister," and relates it to a personality that is basically "bold and dashing" (192–193). The fact that Evelina so unguardedly voices all her "improper" sensations suggests not only a natural high-spiritedness, but more emphatically, an Eve-like innocence before the Fall into the "world," an innocence that knows no evil or danger.

Evelina is soon made to learn through her experiences at the so-called "private" balls. In this novel, the ball scenes regain their fairy tale centrality. For girls whose only destiny is to marry a man, the ball is their grand social classroom, as well as their major battlefield. Like Cinderella, Evelina shines and outshines as the mysterious, beautiful lady. However, without the necessary props of royal dress and retinue, her experience during the ball is far from an unmixed happy conquest. Evelina is soon found to be laughing at wrong moments. And, having first refused one young man and then danced with another, she is considered to be either "ignorant or mischievous" (32).

Evelina's humiliation continues outside the ballroom. She is often publicly embarrassed by her ill-mannered middle-class relative Madam Duval and the Branghtons. Later, when she tries to beg pardon for her kinsmen's impertinence in a letter to Orville, the girl finds herself entangled in more confusion and shame. Sir Clement, a reckless worshiper of her, intercepts her letter and forges an answer in the name of Orville: " 'With transport, most charming of thy sex, did I read the letter. . . . I am highly flattered by the anxiety you express so kindly. . . . The correspondence you have so sweetly commenced I shall be proud of continuing' " (239). Evelina is sorely hurt by the frivolously familiar tone and the insinuating language. Clement, taking advantage of her impulsive action, deliberately highlights the impropriety of her taking the initiative to write Orville a letter.

Her perplexity and fear in the maze of social decorum are not unlike her ordeal in Vauxhall gardens. She becomes lost in the dark walks and is repeatedly attacked and insulted by gay and riotous young men. Even the unscrupulous Clement is astonished at her unthinkable appearance: "Is this a place for Miss Anville?—these dark walks!—no party!—no companion! . . . " And because Evelina refuses to explain, he half-mockingly, half-threateningly asks her "to suffer" him to make his own interpretation (184). A similar incident occurs in another public garden when the Branghtons bring her to see the fireworks. Once again lost and frightened, she falls into the company of two prostitutes. This time she has to clear her name before a man she cares for a great deal—Lord Orville. Both accidents epitomize her situation in life: living in a baffling world ruled by *others*, she can neither control her actions nor the "meaning" of them, despite her innate innocence. She begins to learn of the traps and dangers lurking in life for defenseless girls like her.

Her tone now changes. After her second frustrating garden adventure, she describes herself: "Listless, uneasy, and without either spirit or courage to employ myself, . . . I indolently seated myself at the window" (222). Back at Berry Hill, she writes to a friend about her obedient return to Villars: "should I *not* else have been the most ungrateful of mortals?" And she reasons with herself, "to be so loved by the best of men,— should I *not* be happy?—Should I have one wish save that of meriting his goodness?" (237–238, my emphasis). It is not the melancholic sentimentalism, "the heaviness of heart," that is new in her voice, but rather her indirect way of speaking, and the stunning consciousness of the gap between what she *should be* and what she *is*. The prevailing negative mode of expression marks her complete alienation, even from her own instinctive feelings. Instead of saying "I am miserable," she questions: "should I not be happy?" Without complaining of the dreariness of Berry Hill, she approaches the subject from a very different angle: "what have I to write? Narrative does not offer, nor does a lively imagination supply the deficiency" (244). Evelina is no longer the garrulous girl who wants to jump onto the theater stage and openly regrets she has missed a chance to meet Lord Orville in the street. Even her girlfriend finds reason to accuse her of "mystery" and "reserve" (238); and Mr. Villars—whom she names as "the dearest, the most venerable of men" (237)—is extremely disturbed by her doubled watchfulness and evasiveness. She admits that she has been suppressing her unhappiness "so much and so painfully in the presence of Mr. Villars" (238). Such passages take us back to our discussion about "fear": clearly, Evelina's altered writing style reflects her recently generated sense of fear and a new knowledge about the truth of her own social situation. And her growing alienation from the fatherly Villars marks her final maturity. She seems to have realized, through her painful experiences of *being interpreted* and Villars's frequent teachings about a woman's reputation, that for all his kindness, Villars stands for a moral and social order that rules, judges, and punishes. Now she becomes very careful, in her evasiveness as well as in her measured trustfulness. She never hints at any unhappiness with Berry Hill, but she lets herself become "very ill" (250)—even after she has confessed to Villars her upsetting exchange of letters with Orville and supposedly has regained her spiritual tranquility. Consequently, the old man has no choice but to let her go again to recover her health.

In this sense Evelina's "progress" entails a "fall"—a fall from original innocence and fearlessness into experience and the accommodation to the social norm.[2] It is as though she realizes that her ephemeral role as a striking, mysterious beauty falsifies her true position in life, and so now she chooses a new place— the window. She retires to the window after the depressing night in the London gardens, and while staying with the embarrassing Branghtons, she often sits by "very quietly on a window" (197). She preserves this habit when she is again at Berry Hill: "I walked to the window. I believe I remained near an hour in this situation" (245). Later, when she is once again with her insolent aristocratic acquaintances, she is more self-conscious about her preference for the window position: "Since I, as Mr. Lovel says, am *Nobody,* I seated myself quietly at a window, and not very near to any body" (266–267). Obviously, Evelina has turned her habitual position at the window into a symbolic gesture. The window is a very marginal and very ambiguous place: it is part of the room yet at its very edge; it faces out yet can never reach that wider outer space.

We should note that Evelina's symbolic "self-exile" occurs simultaneously with many scenes of social comedy. It is from her marginalized position at the window that Evelina watches and ridicules. Her comic description is never merely comic, but is interwoven with the self-consciousness of the alienated observer; she makes her window-sitting gesture a kind a social manifesto, announcing her distance from the whole spectrum of social groups around her. Disowned by her aristocratic father and disgusted by the vulgar relatives eager to claim her, feeling inadequate before Villars's moral demands and unsure about her future "master," Evelina is estranged and secretively critical about all. Her window position is a sign of acquiescent acceptance of her marginal place, but an acceptance that is not without bitterness and irony.

Sometimes she purposefully plays up her "nobody-ness"[3] for specific ends: "I took my usual place [at breakfast], and Mrs. Beaumont, Lady Louisa, and Mrs. Selwyn, entered into their usual conversation.—Not so your Evelina: disregarded, silent, and melancholy, she sat like a cypher, who to nobody belonging, by nobody was noticed" (315). The underlining of her desolation and humbleness—together with the subdued, self-pitying narrative voice—is also part of her deliberate maneuvers to secure a social footing. In *Camilla* (1796), a later novel by Frances Burney, we meet with a heroine who does not learn much from her suffering. After too many reconciliations and misunderstandings, she unwisely decides to display her flamboyant merriment to "reconquer and fix" her worthy lover; whereas, as the narrator tells us, a "moment's reflection would have told her, that quietness alone . . . could do justice to the purity of her intentions" (705).[4] With this foil, it is easy to see that Evelina's decision is the correct one. The fact that her narrative is effectively tuned to denote her marginalization and passivity shows her intention to "do justice" to her own purity in the eyes of Villars and Orville. In this light Evelina is much more a "heroine" than Camilla, much more a determined shaper of her own destiny.

Burney's contemporaries found the novel very funny: her journals show that her father laughed heartily when reading it, and the coterie around Dr. Johnson highly appreciated the comic picture of Mr. Smith and the Branghtons (Wain 54, 65–66). Perhaps owing to this powerful critical tradition, Burney's "comic flair" (Simons 39) is, it seems to me, habitually overemphasized; many reviewers of today still agree with Walter Allen that "in social comedy" lies Fanny Burney's "true strength" (95). There is, indeed, implied humor when the heroine is presented as speaking in the voice of a lighthearted girl and the gap between the author and the narrator/heroine is distinctly discernible. The keen observations and light satire on ridiculous, vulgar characters do match Evelina's mood at this stage. But as she grows increasingly uneasy and frightened, when the self-pitying sentimental voice takes control in relation to her own "story," the comic scenes gradually become extreme,

gloomy, even violent, burlesques, which tell more than anything else the bitterness of a window-positioned Nobody. As
Ellen Moers maintains, "*Evelina* (and *Cecilia* and *Camilla* as
well) reads much less funny than Burney intended, much more
strained, extreme, fanatic and even frightening in the impossible trials to which the heroine is subjected" (136).

In an article on Gothic fiction Paul Lewis sums up a recent
theoretical approach to "humor" and emphasizes that humor
and fear are at their root connected, since both are caused by
"the sudden awareness of an incongruity" (310).[5] Burney seems
to have intuited this intrinsic connection and relentlessly pushes
the comic to its uncanny extreme. This explains the "violent
farcical actions and characters in *Evelina*," which, as Margaret
Doody says, "are images of what the comedy is about" (48).
"Incongruity" is exactly the word to characterize the droll episodes of violence in the novel, which jar against the mostly re-
fined, genteel narrative voice. A remarkable example is the
practical joke played upon Madam Duval by Sir Clement and
his friend. Though no actual physical injury occurs, there is real
brutality. The carriage is overturned and the old woman, who
falls into the ditch and loses her wig, is frightened to death by
the impersonated robbers. No "vulgarity" of Madam Duval
could justify such treatment. Evelina, who is not only the
granddaughter of the humiliated and ridiculed victim, but also
an equally powerless woman, grows increasingly upset and uneasy about such a "joke." Another notorious aristocratic diver-
sion described in the book is the instance in which two very old
and infirm women are forced into a race. Tellingly, one of the
young coxcombs who arranged the race for fun calls Evelina
"the best *young* woman" in juxtaposition with the "best *old*"
one who has won the contest (290). This casual attempt at witti-
cism indicates, even more than Evelina's kinship to Madam Duval, her actual position in such violent social farces: she is almost
as much an entertaining object as those abused old women.

The horror of such "fun" cuts in several ways. It is not just
a satire on the pain-inflicting behavior of these heartless upper-
class practical jokers (who are supposed to be "gentlemen"); it

also seriously questions their version of "comedy"—since such passages are very much modeled on a "masculine" theatrical tradition (Doody 48). Burney seems to be exposing the gender and/or class bias of a literary form: a comedy can be "comic" and entertaining to some yet absolutely humiliating and painful for others. At the same time, these farcical incidents ruthlessly interrupt and interfere with Evelina's own romance; they sound like a mockery of the genteel "feminine" mode of narrative and of the implicit moral and social assumptions behind such language. A true lady is totally out of place in scenes of cruelty and violence. Her proper language cannot handle them, and her behavioral code offers nothing to cope with such situations.

Burney's Evelina is forced to see and to record. It is through the "matured" narrative voice—that is, the "proper" voice of self-restraint and fearfulness—that such oddly outrageous episodes are narrated. Thus, besides the switch from a lighthearted girlish style to a self-conscious, reserved, sometimes double-talking narration, there is also the marked development from a relatively pleasant, humorous presentation of the world to a more harsh and rasping farce and satire. If the first stylistic change reflects a recognizable authorial intention to show Evelina's "progress," then the second (from comic to satiric) seems to be more an unconscious narrative move that is the inevitable result of a maturing and gradually embittered female sensibility. For Burney, violence paradoxically constitutes a fundamental aspect of the supposedly peaceful feminine life, a configuration of the internal and external turmoil. Those out-of-key, bizarre, and implicitly frightful scenes are an important part of Evelina's, as well as her creator's, vision of the world. In Burney's later novels, the delightful humor—which requires a sense of relative security and superiority—diminishes markedly, and far-fetched accidents, impossible violent actions, and sensational melodramas are more frequently indulged. In *Camilla* a nephew blackmails and tortures his uncle for money—and fun; the heroine encounters a group of threatening young men in a bathhouse on the beach; there is also abduction, elopement, imprisonment, attempted murder, accidental suicide, and so forth. Crude and humorless as most of these events are, they

are the more unbridled and extremist expression of that gloomy
and violence-ridden imagination we occasionally encountered
in *Evelina*.

♣   ♣   ♣

"Prithee," whispered his Lordship, "is that queer woman
your mother?"

"No, my lord."

"Your maiden aunt, then?"

"No."

"Whoever she is, I wish she would mind her own affairs:
I don't know what the devil a woman lives for after thirty:
she is only in other folks' way. Shall you be at the assembly?"

"I believe not, my lord."

"No!—why then how in the world can you contrive to
pass your time?"

"In a manner which your Lordship will think very extraordinary," cried Mrs. Selwyn, "for the young lady *reads*." (253).

The "queer woman" referred to by the nobleman is none other
than the quick-tongued Mrs. Selwyn, who indeed appears to be
a rather strange companion for Evelina, the fine gentlewoman.
Being "a lady of large fortune" (243) and by all appearance a
widow, she is her own mistress. She is definitely not "a favourite
with Mr. Villars," because her understanding as well as her manners may be called, according to Evelina, *"masculine"* (251).
However, her reputation seems to be good enough, and the Rev-
erend is too eager to restore his ward's health to be very picky.
Anyway, Mrs. Selwyn is honored to chaperon the young beauty
to Bristol Hotwell when the latter reemerges from Berry Hill.
And she proves to be quite qualified as a protector. When har-
assed by some impetuous young men, Evelina pleads for help:
"pray, Mrs. Selwyn, *speak for me*" (290, my emphasis); in such
situations the older lady usually rushes to her defense with her
sharp tongue, which is obviously the enemy of more than one
man. Not even Evelina is spared. When she once tries to dodge
Orville, who happens to come to the same place, merciless Mrs.
Selwyn does not let the move pass as innocent modesty. "O rare

coquetry!" the woman applauds, "surely it must be inherent in our sex, or it could not have been imbibed in at Berry Hill." Then, again, "My dear child, did you bring the certificate of your birth with you?" And, at Evelina's puzzled negative answer, she continues, "Why then, we shall never be known again at Berry Hill" (300–301). Taking the place of a male "wit," this lady cannot refrain from snatching every chance to satirize or make a smart repartee.

Mrs. Selwyn, as one of the comic background figures, belongs with the Branghtons to the Fieldingesque part of the novel. But, unlike them—actually unlike nearly all the characters except Evelina herself—she is not a type. Burney's upper-class fops, libertines, and arrogant ladies, such as Mr. Lovel or Lady Louisa, are for the most part roughly drawn stock figures that parade before our eyes without arousing any special interest. Even the most elaborated one of them, Sir Clement, is but the shell of a typical rake without half the psychological depth and complexity of a Lovelace. By comparison, the middle-class characters fare much better. The Branghtons and Mr. Smith, with their distinctive demeanor and tongue, are more or less a novelty in the literature of the time. Their speeches, marked by the introductory exclamation "lord" and sprinkled with vague modifiers like "monstrous," are masterly recorded. Yet in spite of this, they remain "humor" characters: they are—being tasteless, stingy, sometimes excessively humble, sometimes unduly pretentious—the undifferentiated, collective representatives of vulgar manners. Their single dominant trait is so overwhelming and so extravagant that they become overexaggerated and overused caricatures.

Among these secondary characters who can be summarized by a single epithet, Mrs. Selwyn stands out strikingly and surprisingly. She shares with the heroine the "privilege" of being somewhat opaque and ambiguous. If Evelina the narrator reveals her inner complexity mainly by the way she learns to tell her story, then she calls attention to Mrs. Selwyn through her failure, or refusal, to "settle" that woman within the narrative. Mrs. Selwyn drifts outside the moral diagram of Evelina/Frances Burney. The narrative of the novel is symmetrically patterned with neatly contrasting pairs of characters: noble lover vs. ignoble one; good patriarch (Mr. Villars) vs. bad father (Sir Belmont); nice ladies (Lady Howard, Mrs. and Miss Mirvan) vs. vulgar women (Madam Duval, the Branghton sisters). The picture is black and white, with little overlapping or intermediate shading—though Sir Belmont is eventually partly acquitted by the removal of the misunderstandings. The essentially good yet boldly improper Mrs. Selwyn does not belong to this world of fable.

This strong-willed woman performs the function of the fairy godmother for the girl. By taking Evelina out to Bristol Hotwell, Mrs. Selwyn offers her the chance to materialize her romantic "fancy." It is also she who, through persistent efforts, manages to force the girl into Belmont's presence and thus brings about the tearful recognition between the father and daughter. She is more earnestly concerned than nonchalantly ironic when she gives some very sound, common-sensical instructions to the yet nameless Evelina on the vital issue of her marriage: "I advise you by all means to marry him [Orville] directly; . . . the young men of this age are not to be trusted with too much time for deliberation, where [their] interests are concerned" (343). In fact, when she stands up angrily to Belmont on behalf of "the injured wife" and demands "justice" for the daughter (345), she appears more a Fury than a kindhearted godmother.

However, this active, unwomanly woman is not recognized as the fairy godmother in the narrative. Evelina the narrator is very ambiguous about and ambivalent toward her. The male moral mentor, Mr. Villars, clearly disapproves of Mrs. Selwyn's aggressiveness and her "propensity to satire," but nevertheless entrusts her with his fragile treasure—a young virgin. Evelina's own narrative carefully avoids expressing any direct admiration of or even proper gratitude toward Mrs. Selwyn; but at the same time it also refuses to condemn harshly her assertiveness, "her want of gentleness; a virtue which . . . seems so essential a part of female character" (251). In the novel the strongest objection to Mrs. Selwyn's "unbounded license of her tongue" comes, ironically, from Sir Clement. "O, Sir Clement, do *you* object to that?" Evelina is a bit sarcastic. "Yes," answers the man who himself enjoys unbounded license (not only of his tongue): "in a *woman* I do; in a *woman* I think it intolerable" (318). This blatant double standard, though not directly challenged by Evelina, is undoubtedly put into question by her persistent disparagement of its advocator.

If Evelina/Burney is somewhat undecided about how to interpret the fearlessness of Mrs. Selwyn, who pleases herself without caring what other people say and is capable of defending herself and her friends,[6] she is nevertheless fascinated by such possibilities. She seems to know how much the vitality of a narrative, as well as a life, depends on deviation from the norm, and shrewdly introduces Mrs. Selwyn to rescue her story from dullness when Evelina herself becomes increasingly demure and dutiful.

Frances Burney cautiously excludes Mrs. Selwyn from the basic plot. Evelina hurries to deny any blood relation to that "queer woman," and Burney does everything to avoid any direct commitment to such characters. Yet spirited women keep showing up in her narratives—such as the gay and rattling Lady Honoria in *Cecilia* (1782), the sophisticated and aggressive Mrs. Arlbery in *Camilla*, and the headstrong girl, Elinor Joddrel, in *The Wanderer*. And in each case the narrator is usually reserved in judging them. Like Camilla, who maintains to her friendship with Mrs. Arlbery in defiance of the expressed displeasure of her mentor/lover, Burney never gives up her little speculations on these impertinent, strong-willed women figures. Their existence is never necessary to the development of the story—except perhaps in the enlivening effects of their bolder speeches and more colorful personalities. Unlike Charlotte Grandison, whose wit and vigor are under the firm control of her brother (even her marriage is completely engineered by him), these lively women of Burney's are not incorporated into either the plot or the "moral" design of the novel; they are free, dangling, capable of doing something strange and outrageous. They are an extra *addition* to the story, a tentative "what if" appended to a fully completed sentence: *what if* a woman chooses to be a Selwyn or an Arlbery?

Only in *The Wanderer; or Female Difficulties* does Frances Burney finally pass judgment on such insubordinate women. In the person of Elinor, she locates female aggressiveness in the "social disease" of radical individualism and egalitarianism disseminated through the French Revolution. The opaqueness of a Mrs. Selwyn or an Arlbery disappears. Elinor, in her awkward and willful pursuit of individual happiness, is a rude caricature, with certain traits of a Madam Duval. Yet at the same time, she is the most consciously political figure in all Burney's novels, and an eloquent spokeswoman for certain militant points of view. She argues against Harleigh, another Grandison-like paragon:

> "You think me, I know, tarnished by those very revolutionary ideas through which, in my own estimation, I am ennobled. I owe to them that I dare hold myself intellectually, as well as personally, an equal member of the community; not a poor, degraded, however necessary appendant to it: I owe to them my enfranchisement from the mental slavery of subscribing to unexamined opinions, and being governed by prejudices that I despise: I owe to them the precious privilege, so shamefully new to mankind, of daring to think for myself." (159–160)

And in a long conversation with Juliet, she denounces the social institutions and prejudices against women:

> "You only fear to alarm, or offend the men—who would keep us from every office, but making puddings and pies for their own precious palates! . . .
> "By the oppressions of their own statutes and institutions, they render us insignificant; and then speak of us as if we were so born! . . . They dare not trust us with their own education, and their own opportunities for distinction. . . ." (378)

Such speeches might have come from some real "champion of her sex" (152), like Wollstonecraft. It is significant that the French Revolution had forced such radical discourse into the consciousness of conservative women like Frances Burney. Though Elinor appears as a semicomic self-dramatizer in a badly organized story and receives some harsh condemnation from her creator, she is assigned a structural importance never enjoyed by any of the previous "lively ladies." As the rival for Juliet, the persecuted maid, and bearing many traits of a spoiled and self-indulgent stepsister, Elinor is deeply involved in the love triangle, and is the chief debater against the properly orthodox couple—Harleigh and Juliet. She is not only given a forum in which to speak, but also gains from Harleigh some respect (152) and from Juliet some rather warm admiration (380). Actually, Elinor is almost more a *true* sister than an abusive and petty-minded stepsister: she tries to help Juliet and her friend attain their self-dependence and challenges Juliet to rebel against the unjust order: "And you . . . endowed with every power to set prejudice at defiance, and to shew and teach the world, that woman and man are fellow-creatures, you, too, are coward enough to bow down, unresisting, to this thraldom?" (379). Through Elinor, the potential subversive implication of Burney's intractable women comes to light. By rendering Elinoresque discourse in direct clashes, as well as in mutually sympathetic exchanges, with the Harleigh-Juliet line, Burney centralizes the hitherto latent thematic and stylistic dialogue between the submissive female paragon and the strong-willed woman. Such contrast and contention in women's behavior was a point of social controversy of the time, and is, as Gilbert and Gubar assert, an expression of the psychological schizophrenia deeply rooted in all female hearts and writings.

When Hazlitt noted in 1818 that Frances Burney "is a quick, lively and accurate observer of persons and things; but she always looks at them with a consciousness of her sex," there seems in his words as much disparagement as praise. For him this female consciousness is at least a partial limitation. But he is keen-eyed enough to connect this quality to the living conditions of the women of the time. "Women," he continues, "in general, have a quicker perception of any oddity or singularity of character than men, and are more alive to every absurdity which arises from a violation of the rules of society, or a deviation from established custom. This partly arises from the restraints on their own behaviour, which turn their attention constantly on the subject" (Howe 6: 123–124). Indeed, as I have

mentioned before, in all Evelina/Burney's presentations of social manners, which are usually comic, there is always this tacit
yet controlling presence of the observer, whose consciousness,
sentiment, and perceptions—more than the depicted scenes and
conversations—are the implied central subject of the narrative.

Burney's gender consciousness is conveyed in more than one
way. Having astutely grasped the love/fear complex, Burney
in *Evelina* adeptly rewrites Pamela's plot into a distinctly female
adventure. The recurrent notes of anxiety and hope tell for girls
marginally situated like Evelina how "real" and vital such a
Cinderella dream is. Evelina's critical, satiric perception of the
world—as expressed in those absurd, violent episodes about
public embarrassment, social oppression, and discrimination—
are reflections of her acute sense of her own Cinderellean position in society, which, however, cannot be fully contained or
resolved by the seemingly fulfilling ending.

Burney also creates certain "type scenes"[7] in relation to female experience, which are full of power and potentiality.
Among these are the agitating experiences at the balls and the
heroine's habitual sitting at the window. A woman reader could
easily recognize such shared experiences and sentiments. And
thus we see Elizabeth Bennet likewise embarrassed by an aristocratic young man at a ball; and characters as different as Fanny
Price and Jane Eyre take similar likings to the window seat. In
this sense, Evelina's ghost is "alive" in many a later cinder girl
long after she herself has been outshone and partially forgotten.

CHAPTER TWO

Emmeline and the "Designing" Women

No disadvantage could equal those I sustained; the more my mind expanded, the more I became sensible of personal slavery; the more I improved and cultivated my understanding, the farther I was removed from those with whom I was condemned to pass my life; and the more clearly I saw by these newly-acquired lights the horror of the abyss into which I had unconsciously plunged.

—Charlotte Smith

Emmeline, the Orphan of the Castle (1788) came into the world ten years after *Evelina*, but from the hand of an older and much more sophisticated woman. By the time Mrs. Smith started writing her first novel, she was nearly forty, with twelve children born to her, and had suffered greatly from her unfortunate marriage. Smith, like Frances Burney, also prefixes a poem to her novel, but it is addressed to "My Children," instead of the worshiped father figure. It is significant that Smith, in her own voice, chooses to speak in the persona of a grown-up, a mother, a self-reliant person. The reader she has in mind is obviously not so much a judging patriarch as some younger friend or child (a daughter) to be counseled or educated.

Partly due to Smith's authorial stance of taking the independent woman as the desired self-image and an ideal, her heroine is not a conventional, piteous, persecuted maid, although the subtitle of the novel, "The Orphan of the Castle" strongly suggests that Cinderella motif. Young Emmeline has very few illusions about the male protector, the father or the husband; and she is endowed with a mind that seems too sturdy and mature for her young age. In the last volume of the novel, the chief patriarch,

Lord Montreville, and his helper, Sir Richard Croft, together ponder over the skill and resolution with which Emmeline Mowbray claims her right to the family name and property. This cannot be the doing of an inexperienced girl like Emmeline, they conclude. But, there is her friend Mrs. Stafford, who is, as Sir Richard says, "artful and designing and intriguing; a woman . . . who affects and pretends and presumes to understand and be competent and equal to business and affairs and concerns with which women should never interfere or meddle or interest themselves" (432).

Sir Richard's repetitious use of several groups of synonyms ("designing and intriguing," "affects and pretends and presumes") with increasing gravity reveals his aggravated impatience with this female's attempt to manage her own affairs. And his accusation is not totally off the point. Between the three main women characters, Emmeline, Mrs. Stafford, and Lady Adelina, there is close friendship and cooperation, which does in a way damage or disrupt the existing order embodied by Lord Montreville. On the surface, the number-one heroine, Emmeline, is impeccably proper and prudent. She and her friends are, like Pamela and others, the victimized innocents. Emmeline is the victim of the passion of her cousin Delamere and the ambition of his parents: the former plagues her and presses her to elope, while the latter hound and menace her, trying to prevent such a "disaster." Mrs. Stafford and Lady Adelina are both miserable in their married life. Mr. Stafford always gets his family into dire financial plights with his whimsical plans and projects. Adelina Trelawny, on the other hand, is repulsed by her hard-drinking husband and forms a fatal extramarital attachment to a reckless and fashionable young man named Fitz-Edward. When depicting their experiences, Smith uses terms expressing fear, as if the author, like *Evelina*'s, wants to emphasize the defenseless situation of the women and their natural weakness. In Chapter Twelve of Volume Four, in which an unexpected meeting between Adelina and Fitz-Edward happens, within ten pages the words "terror" and "terrify" appear over ten times, plus many "alarm's," "dread's," and "fright's." Yet, for all their advertised helplessness and fearfulness, these women, at least Emmeline and Mrs. Stafford, rouse some sentiment other than pity.

In a way, Charlotte Smith's women are very competently, even aggressively, self-protective, if not self-sufficient. Unlike Pamela, Emmeline never loses her self-control or faints, even when words like "terror" pop up two or three times per page. Among the three bosom friends, one engagement is broken and two marriages split up, a husband and an ex-fiance are killed, and another husband exiled from his family and the denouement of the story. With their joint efforts, they reestablish Adelina, who is, according to the accepted view of the time, an adulterous, fallen woman, in the house of her rather strict and righteous brother; and, with good luck and the help of some male friends, they recover Emmeline's legitimate name and inheritance. Eventually Mrs. Stafford herself also benefits financially from her friends' good fortune. Judging from these bare facts, they seem almost a self-serving clique, a far cry from timid and fragile "angels."

Emmeline, the exalted heroine of this novel, is a disturbingly alert businesswoman in the transaction of love and marriage; and Delamere, the tragic lover, is systematically deflated. As a true romantic, Delamere dutifully worships beauty and refuses to trade love for monetary or political interests. Defying the "selfish ambition" of his parents (51), he insists on marrying his cousin Emmeline, a penniless, illegitimate orphan. However, even this generous, ardent love cannot daze the sober eye of Emmeline. Somehow she manages to foresee danger in the willfulness and spoiled character of her admirer, and to keep her emotional distance from her impetuous cousin. When her intention of breaking her engagement with Delamere is made known, Lord Westhaven, a respected relation, expresses his worry that the latter might not survive a total rejection. Emmeline summons Rosalind's famous lines for her own defense: "Men have died from time to time, and worms have eat them— but not for love." However, without the note of affectionate tease, without Rosalind's youthful and flamboyant passion that underlies her utterance, these words somehow grate upon the ear of the listener. Removed from its original context, this piece of "realistic" truth becomes false to a large degree: poor Delamere does *die* for his unlucky love in the end. No wonder even an unbiased bystander like Westhaven speaks of Emmeline's dismissal of her hapless lover as "very inflexible" and "very cruel" (408–409).

It is highly doubtful whether Emmeline ever loves any man, even her chosen Godolphin. She compares Delamere's "unjust suspicions," "haughty reproaches," and "long, indignant anger" with "the gentleness, the generosity of Godolphin" (364). She surely sees in the latter a safer husband and companion. But, if we take losing one's mind—at least a little—as an index of love, then Emmeline definitely betrays no such symptom. "I most ardently wish Lord Delamere well," she is candid and confident in putting forth her own principle, "and would do any thing to make him happy—*except sacrificing my own happiness*" (403, my emphasis). Delamere has to be sacrificed, Emmeline's speeches suggest, if *his* will for fulfillment happens to clash with *hers*. The author seems determined to shun no cruelty inevitably entailed in the struggle for individual survival and happiness: it is a kind of Darwinian war that goes beyond personal good will or hatred.

Emmeline's cool-mindedness and circumspection in this fight is almost astonishing. She has seriously reflected on the project of elopement and clandestine marriage proposed by Delamere:

"If I marry Delamere contrary to the consent of his family, who shall assure me that his violent and haughty spirit will bear without anguish and regret, that inferior and confined fortune to which his father's displeasure will condemn him? His love, too ardent perhaps to last, will decline; while the inconveniences of a narrow fortune will encrease; and I, who shall be the cause of these inconveniences, shall also be the victim. . . . To whom can I then appeal? Not to my *own* heart, for it will condemn me for suffering myself to be precipitated into a measure against my judgment; nor to *his* family . . . and I have *no* father, *no* brother to console and receive

me, if he should drive me from him as impetuously as now
he would force me to be his." (150–151)

This is very much in the tradition of Pamela's deliberation on
the fate of a "vile" kept mistress, but more focused on the calculation of happiness. With Emmeline, no cardinal issue like chastity is actually at stake, since she is quite sure of Delamere's
sincerity and honorable intentions. What she wants is "insurance" for her emotional investment; as she asks, "who shall assure me?" Her style, more than Pamela's, resembles that of
business accounting, carefully examining the balance sheet and
the possibility of gain and loss.

Once decided on the unacceptableness of Delamere's proposal, she initiates a number of diplomatic moves between Delamere and his father, her uncle Lord Montreville. Do not push
too hard, she keeps warning the young man, giving him just
enough hope to prevent him from doing anything rash and desperate. At the same time, she gives her solemn promise to her
uncle that she will never marry his son without his permission,
in exchange for his agreement to desist from coercing her into
marrying a loathsome old banker. Through such negotiations
Emmeline gets things very much into her own hands: she se-
cures a hundred pounds a year from Montreville and maintains
her right to meet the young lover. Sometimes this double compromise borders on double betrayal—she often informs Montreville of Delamere's newest maneuver, almost as though she
deliberately uses the father to fend off some of the son's undesir-
able advances and "brandishes" the son's reckless passion to
threaten and control the father. Yet everything is done in the
name of virtue and integrity. She makes no secret of her con-
tracts with either side, and thus enhances, instead of damages,
her honor and credibility by fulfilling them.

In this dazzling performance of tightrope-walking, Emmeline
shows not only a maturity far beyond her age, but also the aggressive virtue of prudence. Not that passion or indiscretion is in
any sense an unforgivable sin in her and her creator's eye. Adelina
is "guilty" of both, yet she has quickly won the ready sympathy
and help of Emmeline and Mrs. Stafford, the two model women

of the novel, and is promised a happy future with her morally improved lover.[1] Nevertheless, virtue and rationality are prescribed as the best policy, as Emmeline has learned from the unhappy married life of Mrs. Stafford and Adelina. Adelina's extreme distress—forlorn, destitute, and pregnant with the illegitimate child of Fitz-Edward—must certainly have been intended, by the mother-educator-like writer, to be a solid lesson for Emmeline, and all female readers as well, about the danger of romantic involvement and the unequal punishment facing different sexes for moral slips or social transgressions. It is only natural that Emmeline determines to take good care of herself and not become the easy prey of some wanton boy's flitting whim.

Perhaps no man would like to have such a domestic politician—inside or outside his house. If unbridled passion is not to be condoned, then such candid and self-righteous utilitarianism in women is surely more upsetting for men as the ruling sex. Interestingly, for all Emmeline's sobriety, a contemporary reader, the radical feminist Mary Wollstonecraft, still finds in the novel too much sentimental romanticism and love fantasy. She is worried that Adelina's amorous adventure might generate in young women "false expectations" and dissatisfaction with "the moderate and rational prospects of life" ("Review" 333). Actually, if young Wollstonecraft had not been so overanxious about the dangers of the romance, she might have recognized a "comrade" in Mrs. Smith,[2] who makes her protagonist an absolute rationalist. Adelina's entangled love affair, although having in a way opened a little back door for romantic adventure, serves on the whole as a complementary footnote to Emmeline's extremely sensible and well-calculated behavior. Mrs. Smith's rationalism is completely secular and pragmatic, without the sparkling idealism of Wollstonecraft that is rooted in a kind of religious fervor (no matter whether she is a religious "believer" in the old sense or not). In its quiet way, Smith's secular individualism is more mature and even more disruptive. Wollstonecraft had yet to learn about the sexual and emotional repression she had been propagating and practicing; whereas in *Emmeline,* a positive place is already assigned to passion and sexual love through the character of Adelina, only her suffering suggests how slim the chance and how great the risk if a woman pursues this path in the existing social structure. Emmeline's loyal friendship with Adelina attests that her version of modesty is not quite grounded in a rigid, oppressive code taught by male teachers, but based on a careful weighing of the female interest. Her mind, though a bit tough toward men, and with good reason, too, is very flexible and understanding toward her sisterly friends.

Mrs. Smith's stress on rationality is motivated mainly by the fear of the mental as well as physical damage brought upon women by infectious romantic fantasy, as part of the ideological package peddled to women to make them "merely to gratify the appetite of man, or to be the upper servant, who provides his meals and takes care of his linen" (Wollstonecraft, *Rights of Woman* 126). From this standpoint, when people like Mrs. Smith and Wollstonecraft use terms like "duty," "modesty," "propriety," they have both correctly grasped the individual-istic core of these loudly advocated middle-class moral con-cepts, and instinctively revolted against the patriarchal bias, the double standard, and gender oppression embedded in them. Their dutiful women, instead of being passive, obedient, and fearful, react efficiently in the world to protect and promote their own rights. And that is why those characters are thought to be pushing and "designing" and intolerable, despite the fact that they never do anything improper or speak in the offen-sively sharp, ironical voice of a Mrs. Selwyn.

Sir Walter Scott, a sensitive male reader, correctly discerns in Mrs. Smith's novel an annoying aggressiveness and feminine "selfishness" in relation to man. Sympathetic to the hapless De-lamere, he feels rather uneasy about Emmeline's "prudence": "we cannot help thinking that prudence, as it is in a distin-guished manner the virtue, so it is in some sense the vice of the present time" (2: 61). It might not be fair to say that this criti-cism on the "present time" is totally directed to women—Scott always regrets the disappearance of the old chivalrous spirit. But he seems to be much less disturbed when his moderate young hero, a Waverley or an Ivanhoe, timely curbs his interest in some courageous, strong-willed maiden and settles down with a docile and insipid blonde wife. In those cases, a nostalgia is preserved, but no "vice" or "selfishness" on the hero's part is specifically emphasized or criticized. Obviously, even for the large-hearted Scott, calculation in a woman is doubly startling, or repulsive. The girl who breaks her engagement to a man seems no longer the innocent and lovable Cinderella.

✤   ✤   ✤

Emmeline went down to the sea side, and seating herself on a fragment of rock, fixed her eyes insensibly on the restless waves that broke at her feet. The low murmurs of the tide retiring on the sands; the sighing of the wind among the rocks which hung over her head, cloathed with long grass and marine plants; the noise of the sea fowl going to their nests among the cliffs; threw her into a profound reverie.
. . . the moon, yet in its encrease, was arisen, and threw a long line of radience on the water. (16)

For a long while, this sorrowful girl, who has just lost her only friends in the world—two old family servants—and is very worried about her own future, forgets "all her apprehended misfortunes" (16) in the bosom of nature.

Such a lyrical description of the natural landscape in a novel was a new literary phenomenon in 1788, and some critics think it was an invention of Mrs. Smith (Allen 98). A poetic glorification of nature must have been very much in the air then, partly as a re- action to the rapid process of industrialization and urbanization. After all, the publication of *Emmeline* occurred only a decade be- fore *Lyrical Ballads* (1798). However, the image of nature in Em- meline's eye differs significantly from that for a male romantic. Wordsworth wrote in his famous "Tintern Abbey":

. . . Therefore am I still
A Lover of the meadows and the woods,
And mountains; and of all that we behold
From this green earth; of all the mighty world
Of eye, and ear—both what they half create,
And what perceive; well pleased to recognize

In nature and the language of the sense
The anchor of my purest thoughts, the nurse,
The guide, the guardian of my heart, and soul
Of all my moral being. (102–111)

Nature is for Wordsworth essentially something perceived, appropriated, or recreated through man's senses and/or language, inscribed with *his* moral ideals and metaphysical contemplations. For Emmeline and many other heroines, nature is first and foremost a sanctuary, an independent, self-sufficient existence, under whose protection they can escape real abuse and oppression.

Contrasting to the free space of nature are male-dominated buildings. Ironically, "houses" are nominally perceived as women's "domain." It is, however, exactly because middle-class women are doomed by their anatomy to be "house-keepers" for their fathers, brothers, and husbands, that a "house" marks their confine as well as their destiny. Hence this subtle, metonymical uneasiness toward the house in women's novels, which are saturated with an abhorrence of the enslaving social role assigned to women,[3] is a female sentiment not often perceived and depicted by male writers. Even the notorious female penchant for romance and fantasy is an expression of discontent with the domestic space in the house. In the stunning adventures of Emily in Ann Radcliffe's *The Mysteries of Udolpho*, houses and castles always harbor danger and terror, or are used for imprisonment; the only exception is her *lost* parental home, which is in itself part of the Eden-like nature. In that book the presentation of new landscapes is linked to and modulated by the heroine's traveling.[4] In a sense, each new verbal picture of natural scenery implies the expansion of Emily's world, which, though it entails new danger, does enrich and enhance her knowledge and experience. In the subconsciousness of a passionate wanderer like Jane Eyre, a house can also symbolize prison and an oppressive social structure, which has to be burned down before any relatively equal and satisfying relationship between the sexes is possible. "Realistic" girls like Evelina and Fanny Price would stick to their marginal place at the window, looking out from time to time. Emmeline is never quite at ease within a house: for her, in the house there is always inimical power at work, such as the power personified by her uncle Lord Montreville or his lawyer Sir Richard. Once young Delamere asks his father "whether his charming cousin was always to remain a *prisoner in her own room*" (29, my emphasis), to which Lord Montreville gives a blunt, positive answer. Clearly, for his lordship, using the house to encage his niece and thwart the troublesome love affair between the young cousins is not only convenient, but entirely natural and lawful. Though the concept of life as prison is an old Christian idea (Qualls 5–6), in these novels the "imprisonment" that women suffer from is at least as much literal and physical as it is spiritual or metaphorical.[5] What has been forced upon them is tangible injustice, torture, and incarceration.[6]

Going further than many of her sister-writers, Charlotte Smith provides her heroine with more possibilities than just looking out of a window. She allows her go out, to the woods, hills, and seaside. And things happen there. Early in the novel, soon after the woeful Emmeline goes into the woods with a book in hand, she is seen by Delamere, who immediately seizes the chance to proclaim his violent love for her. Later, on the beach of Swansea, she accidentally meets Mrs. Stafford, who becomes her best teacher/friend. Again, while they are wandering in the forest, the two friends discover in a cottage another unhappy beauty desperately in need of help—Lady Adelina near her lying-in. This pattern is so reinforced by repetition that we expect something to happen when Emmeline goes out for a walk during her stay in Switzerland. And we are not disappointed. The tranquil beauty of Lake Geneva does not fail to conjure up the true gentleman/lover Godolphin. Their unexpected meeting ends in a long tête-à-tête, in which the reserved young man finally confesses his admiration for her. In this way, the "outside," nature, is systematically posited as the contrast and the alternative to the "inside," the civilized patriarchal space.

Simone de Beauvoir persuasively points out that in the male-centered cultures, nature itself is conceived of as being female and presented as "the Other"—to be conquered and possessed, just like women.[7] There is, consequently, in women a congenial feeling toward nature, which seems for them both a reminiscence of the lost paradise and a free space that can yet be one's own. But the outside world in *Emmeline* is something much more powerful than the still-life scene an Evelina or Fanny Price could see through the frame of a window. It is a magic sphere, where wish-fulfilling wonder is enacted—it is more than just feminine, it is maternal.

Margaret Homans remarks that "women writers articulate thematically a daughter's bond to and identification with a vulnerable or vanished mother (often figured as Mother Nature)" (16). In *Emmeline*, nature functions as the combination of the hearth and the fairy godmother of the original Cinderella tale, which can console and help the young heroine with a magical power.[8] Mrs. Radcliffe in *The Mysteries of Udolpho* also makes the point very overtly. Whenever the persecuted heroine turns her eye upon beautiful scenery, her heart returns to the home of her peaceful childhood, and the benevolence of nature never fails to comfort her (e.g., 114–115, 120, 209). Considering that in many versions of the Cinderella tale other than Perrault's, the embodiment of this benevolent magic power is some natural object—a red cow, a hazel tree, a fish, etc., which is usually in one way or another related to the dead mother—this presentation of nature as an ally and a wonder-making godmother is not only a quiet female romantic rebellion, but a continuation of the true spirit of the folk traditions.

In this context, it does not at all surprise us that Adelina, being extremely weak and low after her confinement, should ask Emmeline to go out for a walk with her. She always feels the weight of the unspoken reproaches of her upright brother Godolphin and dreads her dismal future as a repenting woman who has forfeited her chastity. This is a world in which a man can raise a natural child without any substantial damage—that is exactly her brother's plan for her newborn boy—while Adelina, if she wants to live in the society at all, will never be able to claim her own son openly. She is so humiliated and depressed by her own devaluation that when Fitz-Edward, the father of her illegitimate baby, asks for her hand in marriage after her husband's death, she says, "I am not worthy the honour of being your wife" (505)! Thus, "going out" is for Adelina a symbolic escape, propelled by a desire for open space and new possibilities. "The wind blew chill and hollow among the half stripped trees, . . . and the dead leaves rustled in the blast" (477). Bleak and chilly as the winter landscape is, it nevertheless teems with opportunities forbidden in Godolphin's house. The man who has been lurking outside, hoping for a glimpse of Adelina, is none other than her guilty lover. The meeting, of course, proves to be of crucial importance for Adelina: seeing with his own eyes Adelina's suffering and her unfailing tender care for him, Fitz-Edward finally makes up his mind to marry her.

An immediate, and remarkable, consequence of the encounter between the lovers is that the girl relapses into insanity. While Godolphin and Fitz-Edward are exchanging bitter accusations, Adelina, hallucinating that her lover has been killed in the duel, deliriously implores Godolphin to take care of her son:

> Lord Westhaven [her elder brother], you know, is coming; and you have promised that he shall not kill *me*. I may however die; . . . for since this last sight I am strangely ill. You and Emmeline will take care of my poor boy, will you not? Had Fitz-Edward lived—nay do not look so angry, for now he cannot offend you—had poor Fitz-Edward lived, he would perhaps have taken him. But now, I must depend on Emmeline . . . (483)

The scene and the speech are brimming with tear-jerking sentimentalism. Although since Marlowe's Turkish queen and Shakespeare's deranged Ophelia, the madwoman is already a stock figure in literature, Mrs. Smith's Adelina still sounds genuine and touching. In her madness, she has given voice to her most deeply repressed feelings, feelings that otherwise would scarcely have ever been acknowledged by herself or her creator—her antagonistic fear of her righteous brothers and her "ignominious" love for her partner in the crime of adultery. This is just one of the outbursts of the terror that "has incessantly pursued her" (278). In a former fit caused by the unanticipated appearance of Godolphin, she fancies that her brothers intend to kill her and take away her son. She deplores Godolphin's cruel austerity: "he will be my judge, and sternly will he judge me—he will forget that he is my brother!" (280).

Madness in literature is often a kind of liberation of the innate nature from civilized restrictions. It is not by sheer coincidence that the literary representation of a madwoman is usually connected with a sense of freedom and naturalness. Marlowe's mad Queen Zabina suddenly breaks up the eloquent, iambic Marlovian lines, and cries in broken prose about liquor, milk, fire, blood, her child, the setting sun, and the streamers (5.2. 247–257). With its simple wording, homely images, conversational style, and illogical free association, her speech forms a contrast to the dominant pompous language of ambition and splendor. If Zabina's broken words reveal a "naturalness" mainly through her style, then Ophelia's mad scene and her subsequent death, which is developed around the image of flowers, point to a symbolic reunion with nature. Even without the help of modern psychology, it is not difficult to see how lunacy opens up a new linguistic as well as a spiritual space for these women. Otherwise, with a father constantly moralizing, a brother vigilant about her reputation, and an extremely sensitive lover who is of royal blood, it is unimaginable how Ophelia could ever speak her true mind, let alone sing a bawdy song about the maid of Valentine's Day. Similarly, insanity offers Adelina and her author a serviceable linguistic liberty, which is used to condemn the perfectly "kind" and "just" representatives of patriarchal order (Lord Westhaven and Godolphin) and to allow the "fallen woman" to assert her dignified natural desires openly.

In his book *Reading for the Plot* Peter Brooks regards desire/ambition as a kind of impetus for all novelistic narratives: "Ambition provides not only a typical novelistic theme, but also a dominant dynamic of plot: a force that drives the protagonist forward . . . " (39). The Cinderella plot, as I have repeatedly demonstrated, is essentially a narrative about female desire and ambition.

In folk tales, a heroine's desire is seldom conveyed by her conscious wishes; usually it is expressed through what she lacks.[9] At the beginning of the story, a typical Cinderalla is, as a rule, placed under worse circumstances than an ordinary woman—that is, she suffers not only from symbolic castration, the powerlessness destined to all her sex, but is also subjected to additional destitution and abuse. So, when Emmeline Mowbray first appears on the scene, she is an orphan without a legitimate name, who—worse than the case with Evelina—has no protector, no friends, and "no power to procure for herself the necessaries of life" (6). To gain all these—property, protection, and name—is, understandably, her task and her "ambition." Because of the numerous previous texts that were based on the same pattern, the reader will not fail to recognize the heroine even at this early stage and expect the happy marriage, which is bound to happen on the last page and is the only conceivable way of fulfillment.[10]

The narrative of *Emmeline* deliberately alludes to and reflects on its pre-texts, which reveals an unusual critical concern about the plot itself. Nearly all the young women in *Emmeline*, be they aristocratic or plebeian, are avid novel readers. Delamere's younger sister Augusta is "deeply read in novels . . . and having from them acquired many of her ideas" (71). Consequently, she reads her brother's love for Emmeline as a living romance and secretively promotes it. Daughters of a rich bourgeois widow, the Ashwood sisters are even more ardent and unashamed about their daydreams, which originate in popular fiction. They constantly talk about "delicate embarrassments and exquisite sensibilities," want to cultivate "sentimental friendship," and long for their Prince Charming (some knightly young lord) who will carry them away and marry them "in despite of all opposition" (229, 507). Mrs. Stafford and Emmeline, the two most sane and intelligent women, are also found sitting quietly and attentively listening to Fitz-Edward reading Frances Burney's *Cecilia*.

Such references pose two questions, which sometimes cross, even merge into, each other. First, what place does the literature of romantic love occupy in the mechanism of the heroine's desire? And secondly, what is the relationship of this particular novel to these acknowledged pre-texts?

The vague Cinderellean dream of the background figures in *Emmeline* is not exactly the expression of the dominating "erotic wishes" that Freud assigns to women (47). The giddy Ashwood girls want, more than a husband/master, an exciting life. Their awkward efforts to form a "sentimental friendship" with Emmeline, or their vain wish to leave letters "to edify the world" (507), are superficial imitations of Pamela-like fictional protagonists: they want to be "heroines." Only in them, as in most women of their time—perhaps even of ours—social ambition takes the form of a love dream. Nancy Miller is right in trying to rewrite Freud's formula, and to argue that there is an "ambitious wish" underlying every erotic romance of female daydreams (40). And, as the cases of Augusta and the Ashwoods show, books, especially novels and romances, are among the major disseminators of such desire. These books plant in the hearts of young women a dissatisfaction with their present lives—they see themselves as the neglected, even ill-treated cinder girls—and build up expectations for the future. When Charlotte Smith writes in a personal letter that the more her mind expanded through reading books, the more she "became sensible of personal slavery" (Scott 2: 32), it is likely she is not referring to love romances. However, she has touched upon the notable fact that books, whether romantic fiction or more intellectual ones, offer a criticism or an alternative to the status quo, and thereby deepen and intensify whatever discontent the readers feel in their lives. Even for the mild and seemingly smooth-sailing Augusta, her love for novels and her cryptic sympathy for Emmeline signify a personal dissatisfaction with her life and a quiet rebellion against her parents.

Secondary characters like Augusta and the Ashwoods represent a pattern of desire that I would call "the implied primary pattern." It is "primary" in the sense that in this novel it is something given and to be judged and reacted upon. The descriptions of these "romantic" girls, though sketchy, tell enough for us to both recognize the desire (the Cinderella dream in a broad sense) and to identify its source (the novels based on this plot). The fact that narrative plays the role of the "mediator" in the triangular structure of desire and reproduces its own pattern in the reader's mind is of cardinal importance.[11] It testifies to what degree the private desire is socially dictated and socially mediated (at least as the novelist perceives it), and explains why women writers like Mrs. Smith, Wollstonecraft, and Austen find it necessary to comment and recomment on the enchanting plot.

Such a "primary pattern" forms the background against which Mrs. Smith unfolds Emmeline's story, which constitutes a kind of "revised pattern." That the ambition of a girl can only take the form of a typical romantic love story is a matter of course for the Ashwoods, but it is not so certain and indisputable for Emmeline and her best adviser Mrs. Stafford. The happily-ever-after married life becomes suspect—since two of the three central female characters lead miserable lives with their husbands. Throughout the novel, more narrative energy is spent on Emmeline's efforts to avoid one dangerous romantic commitment. The true gentleman who is to win Emmeline's love does not appear until the book is half over. The violent and pathetic death of Delamere is by far more emphatically treated than the happy wedding at the end, which is perfunctorily related in a few sentences.

The romantic dreamers like the Ashwood sisters are caricature figures, and their way of novel reading is ridiculed and criticized. Augusta is fondly talked about, but her cherished "plot" for Delamere and Emmeline goes awry. Her brother's infatuation turns out not to be a happy romance, as she imagines, but a painful tragedy. If the Ashwoods see in romantic love female fulfillment, then Emmeline seems to share many of Mary Wollstonecraft's suspicions that such fantasy will most likely lead to bitter disillusion and/or domestic enthrallment.

The treatment of the Cinderella plot (or, in less specific terms, the female dream of romantic love) in the novels is almost always divided. While Richardson offered it as a form of female self-realization compatible with and contained by the Christian spirit and patriarchal order, Fielding exposed and satirized its egoistic pursuit, and Goldsmith, in *The Vicar of Wakefield*, related such alluring illusion to vanity and silliness.[12] With women writers, the narrative pattern is both more eagerly affirmed and more fiercely criticized. The exploration of the new imaginative frontiers opened up by the plot is haunted by the awareness of the sharp discrepancy between its fairy tale promise and the actual dim and cramped living space facing most women. The most detrimental suggestion of such a story, as some radical feminists like Wollstonecraft assert, is that a woman is destined merely for marriage.[13] Due to such inherent ambiguity of the narrative pattern, the cultural support or condemnation of the theme of romantic love from either sex is, and has to be, halfhearted.

A love/hate relationship with the stereotypic pattern is characteristic of the best works of this subgenre. All worthy Cinderellean heroines, from Evelina to Jane Eyre, without exception fight strenuously against the beguiling dream, yet every one of them eventually has her romantic wish realized. In the same way, Mrs. Smith makes her heroine evade the trap of an imprudent romance and questions matrimony as the gate to happiness and meaningful life in the narrative convention, and yet firmly anchors her story on marriage. She does this not only because she belonged to a generation too much shaped by and immersed in the literary tradition to be totally free from it; but also because she was instinctively aware of the pros and cons from a kind of feminist point of view.

Thus we see in *Emmeline* a continuous effort to revise the Cinderella story. What we have discussed in the last two sections—the prudent yet strong-willed woman as the hero in place of the naive, virtuous, and sentimental girl, and the systematic presentation of nature to convey female wishes and inspirations—are two of the major revisions. Another one is the forceful stretching of the plot itself. Wedged into the overall narrative of a cinder girl journeying toward marriage with a paragon gentleman are the lengthy digressions about the struggling women—Adelina and Mrs. Stafford—as well as the embarrassingly painful story of the Emmeline-Delamere relationship, which is an account of prolonged resistance and escape.[14] It is not nice Godolphin, but rash, vehement, and finally rejected young Delamere who is the central male protagonist.

In this light some willful characterizations and unlikely coincidences in the narration suddenly come into focus. The characterization of the sensible heroine recast from the dreaming cinder girl is strikingly artificial. In the first chapter of *Northanger Abbey*, young Austen mocks Emmeline-like perfection. Indeed, Emmeline is incredibly faultless: she is dazzlingly beautiful, intelligent, kind, "adored throughout the country," and learns "every thing with a facility that soon left her instructors behind her" (1–7). Blunt and exaggerated as those descriptive passages may appear to a post–Jane Austen reader, they do fit into Mrs. Smith's plan. What she aims at here is not a life-size girl accurately copied from life but a true "heroine," furnished with all the "armor" that her time would allow a woman—beauty, virtue, a prudent, rational mind, and all fine "accomplishments"—so that she may best stand the trials of life. As I have suggested before, *Emmeline* is, more than many other novels, true to the fairy tale spirit of wish-fulfillment.

Equally arbitrary is the way all kinds of incidents are arranged. During her foreign trip, Emmeline meets the former servant of her parents, who provides her evidence of their legal marriage. Through this accidental event she recovers "her name and fortune" (363), and gains nearly all she lacks at the beginning without marrying a "prince." It reminds us that Evelina, too, feels it is important to be recognized by her father before her wedding. Though not as strong a sign as Emmeline's complete financial independence after her long struggle with the Montrevilles (father and son), this conveys a similar wish not to be totally dependent on her future husband. Obviously, what Smith distrusts is not the protagonist's implicit desire, but the *way of fulfillment* proposed by the literary convention. Similarly, Delamere's death, on which the narrative greatly depends, is casually inserted into the story. The duel and the consequent death, though not improbable, are neither properly prepared for in the narrative nor very convincingly presented as the natural end of the character. Rather, it appears simply the easiest way to get rid of an extra lover and an unwanted romance.

Such open neglect of "plausibility" does create what Nancy K. Miller calls "a form of emphasis: an italicized version" (38), which indicates a female wish to go beyond the marriage plot. Miller stresses that the precondition of plausibility is the stamp of approval affixed by public *opinion*, and cites Genette's words to support her point: "Real or assumed, this 'opinion' is quite close to what today would be called an ideology, that is, a body of maxims and prejudices which constitute both a vision of the world and a system of values" (quoted in Miller 36). As a result, she continues, "arbitrariness can be taken as an ideology in itself, that is, as the irreducible freedom and originality of the author" (39). In *Emmeline*, the author's resort to implausibility shows, in a reverse way, the social prohibitions against a poor girl gaining property and respect by herself, or against a "fallen woman" like Adelina escaping retribution. The violation of plausibility carries with it a silent protest, an irrepressible desire for new space and new possibilities.

In this sense, the breach of the respected narrative discipline is a kind of revolutionary *act*. Smith's unashamed, willful way of using unlikely incidents never fails to favor the powerless and unhappy women characters. In addition to the complete release that Delamere's death finally gives Emmeline, Adelina is also saved because of her husband's timely death, presumably from intemperate drinking. If Emmeline's enemies, the elder Montrevilles, desire the absolute privilege enjoyed by the pre-Revolutionary French aristocracy to control their troublesome social inferiors (128), then these miserable women must have been dreaming of miracles that would transfigure their lives completely. In the fictional world of *Emmeline*, Providence is so much on the side of the underprivileged women that various accidents wipe away their tormentors, just as in the French Revolution, which broke out soon after *Emmeline*'s publication, the hierarchy so admired by Lady Montreville was violently attacked. Of course, neither Emmeline nor her creator are radicals like the militant French revolutionaries who could ruthlessly send their oppressors to the guillotine. Yet in a way they are not very far from that. Secretly, they also want to clear the way to freedom and happiness, as the arbitrarily arranged "accidents" in the novel suggest.[15]

From the above discussion we may infer that the narrative emphasis in *Emmeline* is not on the sequence of events that happen to the heroine, but on the comparison between this sequence and the pre-texts, the "primary pattern." In other words, the novel is less interested in Emmeline as a fully individualized person than in the validity of the plot offered to woman by preexisting literature. Emmeline as a character is rather a "laboratory" product—an idealistic device in an imaginary experiment with the possible female lot within the existing social framework.

However, toward the end, the narrative collapses into the old pattern. Although Emmeline has been completely successful in her dexterous dealings with the Montrevilles, and has regained her name and property, she still has her life to live and time on her hands. What else can she do but marry a rational and unobtrusive man who is not very likely to make trouble? Then, as if by a second thought, the narrator in the middle of the story introduces such a young gentleman in Godolphin, who takes care of Delamere at his deathbed and clears up all the emotional mess left by the tragedy.

Until that point, the novel has been fighting against or deferring the marriage as the catastrophe, the ending. Now, as if exhausted by the prolonged struggle between Delamere and Emmeline, the narrative—after the young man's death—quickly falls back onto the beaten track of the marriage plot. The typical pilgrimage is then completed: from a persecuted orphan to a happily married bride, Emmeline is, after all, another Cinderella in the long line of similar heroines.

Emmeline was first published, just about the time that the feminist pioneer Mary Wollstonecraft went to London to become a professional writer and the "forerunner of a new species" (Wardle 164). *Emmeline* arrived a little too early. Though

Mrs. Smith was already considerably alienated from the narrative paradigm, a tentative, Wollstonecraft-like solution outside marriage was yet unimaginable to most people. For all the freedom that is supposed to be enjoyed by the imagination, it seems that as far as plot is concerned, the wildest fancy always drags humbly behind lived experience.

✣ CHAPTER THREE ✣

Fanny Price's Perplexity over Language

> Mrs Elton took a great fancy to Jane Fairfax. . . .
> . . . "Jane Fairfax is absolutely charming. . . . A sweet, interesting creature. So mild and ladylike. . . ."
> . . . "She is very timid and silent. One can see that she feels the want of encouragement. I like her the better for it. I must confess it is a recommendation to me. I am a great advocate for timidity . . . in those who are at all inferior, it is extremely prepossessing."
>
> . . . .
>
> Mr Knightley was thoughtful again. . . . "but not even Jane Fairfax is perfect. She has a fault. She has not the open temper which a man would wish for in a wife."
>
> —Jane Austen: *Emma*

"Nobody falls in love with Fanny Price," Tony Tanner says in his introduction to Penguin edition of *Mansfield Park* (8). Few would dispute Tanner's observation, though most critics agree on the importance of the book in the Austen canon. Somehow Fanny Price seems to resemble the upsetting modern antihero more than a lovely Cinderella. Lionel Trilling believes no one "has ever found it possible to like the heroine of *Mansfield Park*" (128); Kingsley Amis considers her "morally detestable" (142). Gilbert and Gubar are derogatory when they compare her to the subservient Snow White (165), and Mary Poovey sounds objective as she notices that "beside the charming, outspoken Elizabeth Bennet, Fanny Price holds little appeal for many readers" (212). Whether such comments can prove Fanny Price's ultimate "dislikability" is disputable: rather they testify, repeatedly, to the very different, yet enduring artistic fascination of the character. Everyone seems to be wondering why Jane Austen, an author who could produce the most engagingly vivacious characters and cared very much about the reader's response,[1] should choose such a tongue-tied, prudish, weakling to be the focal figure of her most ambitious novel. That, indeed, is a central question that has puzzled many readers of Austen's *Mansfield Park*.

Before coming to the baffling Fanny Price herself, we have to draft a kind of a "chart" for the social dialogues going on between the characters within the world of Mansfield Park, which is the linguistic as well as the moral milieu inhabited and reacted to by our heroine.

According to Marilyn Butler, who deems *Mansfield Park* "the most visibly ideological of Jane Austen's novels" (219), the conversation in the novel is of utmost significance because it "becomes the occasion of the clash of distinctive systems of value" (224). The major clash occurs between the Crawfords and the traditional Bertrams—Sir Thomas and Edmund Bertram. Sir Thomas talks little and mostly makes his existence felt through his absence or mistakes; Henry Crawford is more an "actor" than a serious debater, who is continuously preoccupied with his own performance in idle flirtations and shifting role-playing. Therefore the "war of ideas" between "modern subjectivity and traditional orthodoxy" (Butler 245) naturally devolves to Mary Crawford and Edmund to carry out.

It is a sound critical commonplace that Sir Thomas and Edmund stand for an idealized patriarchy, shored up by the aristocratic order of the English landed gentry and conventional Christianity. Edmund's clerical calling, fully supported by his father, can be read as the crystallization of all their basic outlooks on life. On the other side, Mary Crawford, as a categorical type, appears the radical opposite of the Bertrams' traditional values, and is usually regarded as such. She is an eye-catching contrast to the stereotype of the proper lady: healthy, vigorous, a born rider, a sportswoman, and a quick, bold speaker. She ridicules the respectable professions—the church, the navy, the army; mocks the dignified patriarch Sir Thomas; and has the toughness to poke fun at the situation of her infatuated lover Edmund as the second son. Openly declaring her individualism, Mary says with confident candidness and slight irony: "It is every body's duty to do as well for themselves as they can" (293).

Of course, the Crawfords, especially Mary, cannot be so easily reduced to representatives of a social discourse. Mary is almost all *speech,* like a mask without a face behind it. The author allows us to see very little besides or beneath her fluid and shifting words. She seems to like Edmund, but we never know how much or how little. She sneers at the navy, yet later comes to defend it when she wants to attack clergymen; she pleads for her own selfishness laughingly on one occasion and then denounces that trait in the person of Dr. Grant; she discerns with a quick eye the negligence and abuse that Fanny has suffered in Mansfield Park, but joins in tormenting Fanny with her own self-absorbed behavior. Paradoxically, this quality of all-surface-speech-without-depth makes Mary a complex and individualized figure. Her extraordinary addiction to clever sayings indicates a kind of naiveté. Her thoughtless changefulness and her shifting stance betoken an innocent playfulness and youthful flexibility that have not yet hardened into an utterly practical egoism. As Edmund tries to excuse her, it is "the influence of her companions" that makes her speak in the way she does, sometimes without fully meaning it (275). She is, in a word, imitating a fashionable part in her world, namely, that of a cynical city wit. However, being deprived of silent moments, being presented as completely at ease with her words, Mary becomes, in the end, indistinguishable from the discourse she has adopted.

Thus, in spite of the complications resulting from Austen's sophisticated characterization, the Edmund/Mary dialogue is in its essence the sexually reversed Pamela/Mr. B contention, the key moral-ideological dialectic that energizes the Cinderella plot. Only here the skeptical wit/seducer is an attractive lady, and "virtue, rationality, and self-restraint being tried" are incarnated in a vulnerable, wavering young man.

In the novel their battling discourses are further contextualized, and connected to a map of symbolic social geography.

The more free-thinking and individualistic Crawfords come from London, the urban world of the newly rich middle-class of merchants and professionals; whereas Edmund, the orthodox Bertram, belongs to Mansfield Park, the "stronghold of the old rural Tory values" (Tanner, *Jane Austen* 146).[2] Thus their personal and moral dispute is endowed with a larger social and political perspective. This is itself part of the didactic tradition of the female novel. Both Frances Burney and Charlotte Smith, as I have mentioned before, at times relate their disruptive figures to consequential political issues like the French Revolution, though in very different ways. Jane Austen in one of her high-spirited parodic juvenilian works makes an elderly lady, who is pompously haranguing her niece, allege that the girl's supposed slight of "decorum and propriety" poses a deadly threat to "all order . . . throughout the kingdom" (Beer 170–171). Though in *Mansfield Park* the social implications of the geographical background, like that of the characters, are very subtle and protean, the larger cultural and social conflicts behind the domestic and/or personal tensions are undoubtedly one of the major concerns of the novel.

In accord with a diagram of such clear-cut, dyadic opposition of characters and places, some feminist critics read Mary Crawford as a radical individualist. For Nina Auerbach, "Mary's quest for sisters of gender rather than family, her uncomfortably outspoken championship of abused wives, her sexual initiative, and her unsettling habit of calling things by their names all suggest the pioneering sensibility of her contemporary, Mary Wollstonecraft" (34). Gilbert and Gubar, viewing her as one of the self-assertive, disobedient females labeled as the wicked stepmother (165–166), also confer on her a sort of disruptive force. However, the Crawfords do not signify such a serious break with the Mansfield Park tradition as the above commentaries might suggest. Though lucid diagrams are usually helpful for interpretive reorganization of fictional worlds, they tend to be reductive and oversimplifying. We have to guard against being overwhelmed by our own explanatory scheme, especially with a writer like Austen, who cares as much about the complicated life of individual characters as about the fable contained in the novel. I have tried to demonstrate, in the Introduction to the present study, that within the framework of a Cinderella plot, such polarized factors as individualistic self-assertion and the socially valorized values of female chastity, modesty, and self-denial are at root closely interrelated and constantly interacting with each other. Even in Wollstonecraft, a true revolutionary upholding feminist individualism, we witness an enthusiasm for moral purity, self-sacrifice, and spiritual self-realization, which, though not expressed in religious terms, is in a way connected with the spirit of conventional Christianity and with what Marilyn Butler calls "the traditional orthodoxy."[3]

Besides, Mary Crawford never really means to challenge the established order as her namesake Mary Wollstonecraft once did. It is true that she repeatedly strips the idealized verbal garment off many social practices and flirts with a radically cynical attitude. But, with the protection of ironic distance, she accepts and coexists with what she sneers at, just as she complacently makes use of Dr. Grant's house while attacking him from time to time.[4] Marriage is, she declares, "of all transactions, the one in which people expect most from the others, and are least honest themselves" (79). This deflation of marriage, however, does not prevent her from giving her support to Maria Bertram's mercenary marital arrangement with Mr. Rushworth, or from incorporating her own frankness into the "manoeuvring business" of capturing a desirable husband.

Just as the class line is by no means perfectly distinct in *Mansfield Park*—Henry Crawford is a landlord after all and Sir Thomas has important overseas interests—the opinions of these characters are not exactly oppositional. Actually, Henry Crawford is surprisingly earnest about his estate and landlordship, while Mary, the shiny representative of London, shares many notions with the Bertrams. She agrees with most Bertrams about the "duty" of a young woman to marry money (135, 293, 331) and about the "value of a good income" in general: as she summarizes, "a large income is the best recipe for happiness" (226, 364). She never gets into a direct clash with Sir Thomas. Even in the famous symbolic scene of the wanderings in Sotherton Park, she is not a gate-crasher like Maria, a spoiled Bertram, but has conveniently slid into the park through a side-gate (130). She even once "formally" declares her attachment to the "orthodox" Bertrams: "He [Sir Thomas] is just what the head of such a family should be. Nay, in sober sadness, I believe I now love you all" (354).

What most forcefully bears out the hidden connection between the Crawfords and the "orthodox" protagonists—Edmund and Fanny—are their mutual attractions. Among the four there are three heterosexual love affairs going on, and an intriguing love/hate fascination between the two girls. As Susan Morgan remarks: "With Edmund, and even more with Fanny, it is the Crawfords who most recognize and appreciate their virtues" (61). Ironically, Henry Crawford, the womanizer, is the first who fully realizes the value of quiet Fanny: "the gentleness, modesty and sweetness of her character . . . that sweetness which makes so essential a part of every woman's worth in the judgement of man" (297). And he sees in her "some touch of the angel" (340). These highly conventional views are not so incompatible with the seemingly lawless and free-willed Crawfords if we remember how Mary pays her tribute to the prevailing code from the beginning by saying that "girls should be quiet and modest" (81); and how a typical rake usually practices an overt double standard in marriage and love: doubly fearful of being fooled and cuckolded, he would, in spite of his reveling and debauching, invariably marry a disciplined young virgin. The Crawfords' love for the "goodness" as embodied by Edmund and Fanny, though not so powerful as to suppress for long their other appetites—Mary's aspiration for wealth and social status or Henry's compulsive flirtation—is earnest enough to prove that they are by no means a serious threat to the Mansfield Park order. If there is indeed a freer individualistic ring in their voice and manner, it is more a kind of playful self-indulgence, a spiritual luxury of privileged people.

To sum up, I want not only to underline the connection between, and the common ground shared by, the two sides in the Crawford-Bertram dialogue, but also to point out that in *Mansfield Park* neither discourse is conveyed in its "proper," or idealized, form. Sir Thomas's failure as the patriarch and maintainer of order is so complete that nearly all of his children have gone wrong. In Edmund, who at a crucial moment abandons his own moral stand to take part in the theatrical activity that creates a moral chaos in Sir Thomas's house, we meet with an insipid conventionality that easily breaks down before Mary's coquettish charm. On the other hand, we encounter in the Crawfords, on whom I have focused my foregoing discussion, an individualism that is debased, adulterated, and trivialized.

It is significant that Austen chooses, through these characters/speakers, to present both social discourses in a seminegative way. And it is the insufficient nature of these discourses that gives rise to Fanny's mission in the world of *Mansfield Park*. She is at once the inheritor and the critic of both value systems involved in the Crawford-Bertram confrontation.

Fanny Price's complicated relationship to these two connected yet conflicting social discourses is revealed through her own speaking, which, as most readers feel, is far from enchanting. In his essay "The Two Voices of Fanny Price," Kenneth L. Moler points out that Fanny has two distinctive speaking styles. Double voice or double talk, as some feminist critics assert, is a common female strategy for survival in the patriarchy, and it permeates all literature about women. Cinderella herself is a remarkable "double voicer." When invited to express her own wish, she stammers and recoils, unable to speak the words; yet, to our surprise, when trying to cover her actions, she fluently tells an elaborate lie. What is especially notable about Fanny is not that she speaks in two voices, but the fact that she is at ease with neither.

One of Fanny Price's voices is an unsure "bookish" tongue, "stilted and excessively 'literary'" (Moler 173). By no means a learned or poetic figure, Fanny is the most notorious book-quoter in the Mansfield circle. When the group of young people discuss improving Mr. Rushworth's old mansion house of Sotherton and cutting down the avenue, Fanny appeals to Edmund in a low voice: "Cut down an avenue! What a pity! Does not it make you think of Cowper? 'ye fallen avenues, once more I mourn your fate unmerited' " (87). And, on another occasion, she talks about the chapel in Sotherton:

> "This is not my idea of a chapel. There is nothing awful here, nothing melancholy, nothing grand. Here are no aisles, no arches, no inscriptions, no banners. No banners, cousin, to be 'blown by the night wind of Heaven.' No signs that a 'Scottish monarch sleeps below.' " (114)

Before long we again find her giving another sample of her effusions over nature before a *window*:

> "Here's harmony! Here's repose! Here's what may leave all painting and all music behind, and what poetry only can attempt to describe. Here's what may tranquillize every care, and lift the heart to rapture! When I look out on such a night as this, I feel as if there could be neither wickedness nor sorrow in the world; and there certainly would be less of both if the sublimity of Nature were more attended to, and people were carried more out of themselves by contemplating such a scene." (139)

No touching perceptiveness or fresh impressions are conveyed by such utterances, nor does the narrative provide any vivid background description. In *Mansfield Park,* and in most of Austen's novels, the portrayal of nature is sparse and sketchy, rather different from the works of Mrs. Smith or Mrs. Radcliffe. Though a number of natural scenes are supposed to be sensitively seen by Fanny, rarely are they presented in detail to reinforce her words. As a result, those speeches of hers sound more like purposeful demonstrations of a romantic taste for nature and the old way of life than a spontaneous appreciation of either literature or the real outside world (we can hardly forget that she gets a bad headache after a few hours' work in the garden). Her rhapsodic praise of the night scene, quoted earlier, is rather "unnatural," with its very mannered style, its high pitch, and its exclamation marks, which are by no means in harmony with the celebrated tranquility of the night. Embedded in a social gathering in which Fanny is fated to be a forgotten onlooker, her warm eulogy on nature seems to be more concerned with what is happening inside than what is outside. All expression of human love for nature in literature has as its substructure an implicit social concern, as the pastoral tradition proves. However, with Fanny Price this concern is so urgent that not enough surface attention is paid to nature itself. Her observation that "here's what may leave all painting and all music behind" is to a large degree directed to the upcoming glee of Mary and the Bertram sisters. And her next circuitous move—to invite Edmund to go stargazing with her—makes it very clear that what she cares about most is by no means the outside.

As her proposal for star watching suggests, Fanny is at least half-consciously courting Edmund's attention and appreciation. Looking at natural scenery is, obviously, part of their shared experience. Cowper and Sir Walter Scott are no doubt on the reading list recommended by Edmund to Fanny. "You taught me to think and feel on the subject," she replies when the above-mentioned "window oration" has drawn from Edmund some faint praise (139), shedding light on both the origin of her formal speech style and her motivation for displaying such bookish discourse. In addition to Fanny's own confession, the narrative twice reaffirms the important fact that Edmund has "formed" Fanny's mind (95, 454).

It is clear that Fanny's bookish, poetic language is essentially an echo or repetition of the discourse of Edmund and his favorite writers. Fanny mimics because she wants to please, to win attention and approval. Yet the language is not hers. As the cinder girl at Mansfield Park, Fanny is too socially and sexually self-conscious to identify herself wholly with the assured voice of a male poet. Notably upon such occasions, Fanny always delivers her words "in low voice" (87, 114). This "low voice" is as expressive as any of her actual sayings. Her suppressed voice might signify a worthy effort by Fanny to establish an exclusive intimacy between her and Edmund; but more likely, it is the natural expression of her sense of insecurity and uneasiness. Edmund, who is almost the only listener of all her talks,

is the creator and the judge of her mind, as well as the male
heart she sets out to win. Fanny feels as if she is taking an examination each time she opens her mouth. No wonder she is so
anxious, so rigid and awkward in imitating her teacher's words
and style. What is at stake is the good opinion of her only friend
and protector whom she cannot afford to lose. Fanny never
feels relatively safe unless she speaks something exactly "Edmundian," or something backed up by authoritative quota-
tions.

Most of Fanny's articulations exhibit such an imitative feature. When she does not quote from approved literary sources,
she appeals directly to the patriarchal authority of Sir Thomas,
or Edmund, who, being the male mentor, is a semifather figure. When she laments that the avenue at Sotherton is to be
cut, she sounds anything but a supporter of "improvement."
Nevertheless, when Edmund says that if he had a place to re-
fashion, he would, instead of consigning the work to any "im-
prover," direct it all by himself, faithful Fanny immediately
echoes: "It would be delightful to me to see the *progress* of it
all" (88, my emphasis). Though Fanny's unreserved agreement
with Edmund here might well be based on her sincere belief
that Edmund's version of "improvement" is special and will be
socially and aesthetically praiseworthy, the quick change in her
views on the subject tells her complete dependence on the male
teacher/judge, at least in *words*. Another time, when Edmund
criticizes the moral status of London, Fanny so readily voices
her "certainly" "with gentle eagerness" (121) that Mary Crawford cannot forebear making fun of them. Neither can we forget Fanny's habit of frequently evoking "my uncle," Sir
Thomas. She has adapted herself to her uncle's favorite topics,
such as the question of slavery in America; and she is the only
person who wholeheartedly stands by the side of Sir Thomas
when he puts his foot down about the young people's exuberant
attempt at family theatricals (211). Also, a surprisingly long
oration in defense of Edmund's clerical calling is induced from
Fanny when Miss Crawford, with her cynical tongue and her
usual taunting playfulness, asserts that "a clergyman has nothing to do but to be slovenly and selfish" and gives her brother-
in-law, Dr. Grant, as an example:

"whatever profession Dr. Grant had chosen, he would have taken a—not a good temper into it; and as he must either in the navy or army have had a great many more people under his command than he has now, I think more would have been made unhappy by him as a sailor or soldier than as a clergyman. Besides, I cannot but suppose that whatever there may be to wish otherwise in Dr. Grant, would have been in a greater danger of becoming worse in a more active and worldly profession. . . . A man—a sensible man like Dr. Grant, cannot be in the habit of teaching others their duty every week, cannot go to church twice every Sunday and preach such very good sermons in so good a manner as he does, without being the better for it himself. . . ." (138)

Considering that Edmund's choice of his profession is fully encouraged by his father, Fanny's justification of the vocation is but a sure shot, a safe recapitulation of the "official" Bertram opinion. However, being caught in an ongoing dispute, Fanny has to invent her own arguments on behalf of Dr. Grant. Therefore, she cautiously builds every point on the solid ground of moral banality and impeccable rationalization. Her hesitation and timidity are further manifested by the dominant use of the subjunctive mood throughout her speech, as well as her preference for negative expressions, such as "*not* a good temper," "whatever there may be to wish *otherwise* in Dr. Grant," "*cannot . . . without . . .*," and so on (my emphasis). Such rhetorical devices and the complex sentence structure, which often make her talks so clumsily proper and bookish, unmistakably indicate Fanny Price's discomfort. The rhetorical surface of her language—the stilted style, the grammatically formal syntax, the stock words and images—forms an uncomfortable contrast with the psychological undercurrent of fear, anxiety, and alienation. Austen has wonderfully caught Fanny's uneasiness toward both the act of speaking and the language she has adopted by forcefully underlining the overt mimicking quality of her speeches.

Fanny's other voice is that of incoherence. The best example is, of course, her conversation with Sir Bertram after Henry Crawford has made his proposal to her: "Oh! no, Sir, I cannot, indeed I cannot go down to him. Mr Crawford ought to know—he must know that—I told him enough yesterday to convince him—he spoke to me on this subject yesterday—and I told him without disguise that it was very disagreeable to me, and quite out of my power to return his good opinion." And she continues when Sir Bertram expresses his incomprehension:

> "You are quite mistaken. How could Mr Crawford say such a thing? I gave him no encouragement yesterday—On the contrary, I told him—I cannot recollect my exact words—but I am sure I told him that I would not listen to him, that it was very unpleasant to me in every respect and that I begged him never to talk to me in that manner again.—I am sure I said as much as that and more; and I should have said still more,—if I had been quite certain of his meaning anything seriously, but I did not like to be—I could not bear to be—imputing more than might be intended. I thought it might all pass for nothing with him." (315)

The most striking feature of these passages is the run-on, unfinished sentences, which are loosely and hesitatingly connected by numerous dashes. As Moler says, here "thought is lost and caught up by means of repetition, left incomplete, revised in mid-sentence" (175).

Fanny's "literary" style at once falls into pieces as soon as she is called to speak her own mind. Occasionally, when Fanny is self-righteously angry and not in front of any intimidating male judge/protector, she can give a few impressive sentences that are very much to the point, as when she says to Mary "I was quiet, but I was not blind," or "I cannot think well of a man who sports with any woman's feeling" (358). However, such happy concordance between language and her private mind is rare. Even in such an unusual case, her anxiety about speaking is still too devastating to be borne long. She feels greatly relieved when her talk with Mary is ended: "it was over, and she had escaped without reproaches and without detection. Her secret was still her own . . . " (360). Mostly, when talking about herself, her words are confused and confusing, as in her answer to Sir Thomas. In a letter to Miss Crawford concerning Henry, after a few bumbling lines, she admits: "I do not know what I write" (310). And her long talk with Edmund on the same topic, with its long string of rhetorical questions, is so evasive and misleading that even Fanny herself fears that "she had been overacting caution" (350).

Fanny's confusion here is not generated by any doubt about her own inclination, but by the lack of adequate language that can defend her will. She knows well that all her habitual weapons—discourses of modesty, self-denial, propriety, and rationality—can now be used against her. Henry's offer is considered "desirable" in every sense: he is rich, he is willing to help Fanny's family, and he has conducted his courtship, to use Sir Thomas's words, "properly" and "honourably" (315). In sum, according to the prevailing code, it is Fanny's "duty" to marry Henry Crawford. Even Edmund says that Fanny is not behaving "like her rational self" (344) in refusing Henry.

Her provoked uncle angrily interrogates: "Refuse Mr Crawford! Upon what plea? For what reason?" (316). The only thing Fanny can raise to support her refusal of such a profitable offer is her personal feeling: "I—I cannot like him, Sir, well enough to marry him" (316). Clearly the only language that can justify her is the Mary Crawford-like insistence on personal will. "Selfishness must always be forgiven you know," Miss Crawford says in jest as an excuse for having monopolized the horse and deprived Fanny of her much needed riding exercise, "because there is no hope of cure"(98). Mary openly acknowledges her attraction to Edmund and brazenly claims fellowship from Fanny in speculating about the good fortune that can fall to Edmund if his elder brother dies timely. "Do not trouble yourself to be ashamed of either my feeling or your own," she writes to Fanny about Edmund's chance of becoming "Sir Edmund." "Believe me, they are not only natural, they are philanthropic and virtuous" (423).

Yet, even if Fanny could momentarily unlearn her moral lessons and choose to uphold her right of selecting her own spouse, Mary's discourse of frivolous selfishness would serve her as poorly as Edmund's teachings. Underlying Mary's seemingly dashing candidness is the material backing of twenty thousand pounds. Fanny, the poor dependent relation, would hardly survive another day in Mansfield Park if she were to defiantly proclaim her disobedience and self-will. She cannot even hint at her marriage plot without being considered presumptuous, improper, and sexually aggressive, unless, of course, her love is firmly returned by Edmund himself. Knowing well Edmund's infatuation with Mary, Fanny naturally decides that "she would rather die than own the truth" (317). And she has every reason to feel so.

Fanny halts and hesitates, says and re-says, shifts and evades, because she has no adequate language at her command; and because she is fully aware that she is now asserting herself against her masters. Feeling unable to submit on this crucial point of marriage in the same quiet resigned way as she would give up the pleasure of a dinner party, this mild girl is cornered and must fight. But she well knows that she has to weaken the message, that she is resisting not only the will of one patriarch but the accepted laws of social behavior. Her words are intended as much to hide and confuse as to communicate. No wonder each male listener misreads her according to his own interpretive program. Henry thinks her refusal coyness and is determined to court her more zealously. Edmund infers from her long, misleading explanations that the obstacle is the abruptness and "novelty" of Henry Crawford's address (349–350). Sir Thomas Bertram's angry reproach, though it overestimates Fanny's "rebellion," is nearest to the truth:

> "I had thought you peculiarly free from wilfulness of temper, self-conceit, and every tendency to that independence of spirit, which prevails so much in modern days, even in young women. . . . But you have now shewn me that you can be wilful and perverse, that you can and will decide for yourself, without any consideration or deference for those who have surely some right to guide you. . . . The advantage or disadvantage of your family . . . never seems to have had a moment's share in your thoughts on this occasion. . . ."
> (318)

I agree with Moler's allegation that Fanny's two voices, i.e., her sometimes mannered, overliterary style and sometimes uncertain, stammering way of speaking, are expressions of the same sensibility. However, I would not, as he does, attribute them to Fanny's "school-room mentality" and "moral inadequacy" (173), which are finally overcome through a tough, realistic lesson at Portsmouth. As I have argued, Fanny's two voices first and foremost demonstrate a fundamental ambivalence toward both of the two prevalent discourses, as conveyed in the Crawford-Bertram dialectic, which forms a kind of ideological and linguistic dilemma she never truly manages to transcend.

♣ ♣ ♣

Among a group of merry young people, Fanny appears exceptionally reluctant to open her mouth. For her, "the fairest prospect of having *only to listen in quiet*" promises "passing a very agreeable day" (234, my emphasis). Nearly every character who is somewhat observant wonders at her taciturnity, presuming it should be taken seriously as a meaningful sign. Once Edmund says to Fanny half-disapprovingly: "You are one of those who are too silent in the evening circle" (213). Mary Crawford, soon after her acquaintance with the Bertrams, declares: "I begin to understand you all, except Miss Price. . . . I am puzzled . . . she says so little " (81). Much later, Henry, the other Crawford, tries to decode Fanny's enigmatic silence: "I do not know what to make of Miss Fanny. I do not understand her. . . . What is her character?—Is she solemn?—Is she queer?—Is she prudish? Why did she draw back and look so grave at me? I could hardly get her to speak" (240).

More strikingly than her awkward double voice, Fanny's persistent and resistant silence brings out to what degree she has internalized the Crawford-Bertram dialogue, and how badly she is alienated from both of their discourses. Very early in the novel, we are provided with a fair example of her silent reactions. When the head of the house, Sir Thomas, is called to leave England to straighten out his overseas business, "Fanny's relief, and her consciousness of it, were quite equal to her cousins', but a more tender nature suggested that her feelings were

ungrateful, and she really grieved because she could not grieve"
(66). Succinct as this passage is, it is typical in exhibiting the
two major features that govern Fanny's psychological ferment.
The first is her smoldering hostility and resentment toward the
ruling Bertrams-Crawfords. Nina Auerbach notices this and
names her as "a killjoy, a blighter of ceremonies and divider of
families" (25). Being ever miserable when the whole house is
merry, Fanny can hardly feel happy unless others are in trouble,
as when Sir Thomas is forced to go abroad for financial reasons
or when the elopements of the Bertram sisters throw Mansfield
Park into a mass confusion.

This is not, however, out of an inborn perversity on Fanny's
part, but is predicated by the structural opposition of the interests of people of different castes. Being a paradigmatic Cinderella, a social inferior surrounded by her spoiled "stepsisters,"
Fanny's relationship with them is stereotypically that of conflict
and competition. She has "no share in the festivities of the sea-
son" (69), and naturally finds herself more often hurt than bene-
fited by other people's pleasure-seeking. Thus we have Fanny
morosely watching lighthearted Mary taking from her, along
with her riding horse, Edmund's care and attention: "in Dr
Grant's meadow she immediately saw the group—Edmund and
Miss Crawford both on horseback, riding side by side, . . . the
sound of merriment ascended even to her. It was a sound which
did not make *her* cheerful; she wondered that Edmund should
forget her, and felt a pang" (97–98). In the printed text, the
italics emphatically set *"her"* off, just as in the presented scene
embittered Fanny stands alone on the slope, away from the
"happy party." Evidently, every increase of Mary's gaiety is a
new encroachment on Fanny's very limited happiness, and she
knows this acutely. She resents the mirth of those privileged
people:

> Her heart and her judgment were equally against Edmund's
> decision [to join the theatrical]; she could not acquit his un-
> steadiness; and his happiness under it made her wretched. She
> was full of *jealousy and agitation*. Miss Crawford came with
> looks of gaiety which seemed an *insult*. . . . She alone was

sad and insignificant; she had no share in anything. . . . (180, my emphasis)

Her silent brooding is often a mark of definite displeasure. During an evening party, when she fails to keep Edmund at the window with her attempts at poetic celebration of nature, Fanny perversely remains at that marginal place, refusing to admire the musical performance of the other young ladies. Similarly, in Sotherton Park, she sits alone for a long while, observing with a censorious eye the misbehaved wanderings of all others. During the theatrical and the card game of Speculation, again her obstinate refusal to take part and her baleful silence make her presence almost ominous. Later on, when she soliloquizes in her heart on Edmund's repeated confession of his love for Mary, she sounds almost spiteful:

> She was almost vexed into displeasure, and anger, against Edmund. ". . . He is blinded, and nothing will open his eyes, nothing can, after having had truths before him so long in vain.—He will marry her, and be poor and miserable . . . . Oh! write, write. Finish it at once. Let there be an end of this suspense. Fix, commit, condemn yourself." (414)

This is a long, direct transcription of Fanny's reflection, which, already put into quotation marks, is as lucid and fluent as deliberate spoken words. Remarkably, in such interior monologues Fanny is neither hesitating nor clumsily bookish. On the contrary, she is sharp, straightforward, and has a voice shockingly different from her public ones—a voice of strong passion, of anger, of vengeful impulse, of independent will and wishes. In moments like this, we realize Fanny's spiritual kinship with Mary, just as Sir Thomas sees it in her refusal of Henry's address. Fanny's fascination with Mary is not merely jealousy, but also envy of the daring freedom Mary seems to be enjoying.

Marked by her "other-place-ness," Fanny's existence is a prolonged exile. Wherever she is, she is perpetually homeless: "home is palpable for Fanny only in its absence" (Auerbach 33).[5] Her conscious distancing from social groups, especially the reveling young Crawfords and Bertrams, is not, as I have said before, primarily a moral primness. She has understandably reinforced her anger and mortification with stock from the Sir Thomas-Edmund moral armory, yet her feelings are not generated by rational principles: for instance, all the ethical teachings she has received could not squeeze from her a genuine regret for her uncle's departure. As the narrative takes pains to show, the latent emotional antagonism is firmly founded on the clash of interests. Each pleasure-seeking attempt of the young Bertrams and Crawfords is for Fanny a new deprivation, or at least a heightening of her loneliness, humiliation, and powerlessness. Indeed, the unspoken hatred is so deep rooted and the split remains so unbridgeable, that, in spite of the formulaic happy ending, no scene of forgiveness and reconciliation between Fanny and the stepmother/stepsister figures is enacted in the end. Mrs. Norris, the Bertram sisters, and the Crawfords are firmly, almost overharshly, excluded from the "paradise" of the renovated Mansfield Park.[6] The ending becomes a collective victory of the Prices (of course, only the ambitious ones who have renounced their Portsmouth roots), the humble cinder people: the eventual "disasters" the Bertrams undergo and the consequent "purge" that takes place in Mansfield Park pave the way not only for Fanny's personal gratification, but also for the rise on the social scale of several Prices (William, Susan, etc.).

If Fanny's anger tells more of her Crawford side—her vital awareness of her own interests, will, and feelings—then the fact that she has firmly suppressed this irritation and kept her silence indicates a subjectivity more complicated and circumscribed by environment. Hence the other characteristic that marks her silent reaction to the world is her double response. She often doubts, regrets, even denounces her own hostility toward the Bertrams, who are supposed to be her "benefactors." Having "grieved because she could not grieve" about her uncle's leaving home, Fanny continues to feel the disparity between her feelings and what is "right" and "should-be." "It was barbarous to be happy when Edmund was suffering" (284)—thus goes the narrative, in a passage obviously registering Fanny's consciousness. Just as she often tempers her resentment into a "more softened and sorrowful" feeling (415), she always manages to check her out-of-key happiness. When the Bertrams are trapped in troubles and summon her back from Portsmouth, her first reaction is an immense satisfaction over this revaluation of herself: "To-morrow! to leave Portsmouth tomorrow! she was, she felt she was, in the greatest danger of being exquisitely happy, while so many were miserable. The evil which brought such good to her!" Yet almost simultaneously she senses the impropriety of her pleasure: "She was obliged to call herself to think of it [the Bertrams' trouble], and acknowledge it to be terrible and grievous, or it was escaping her, in the midst of all the agitating, pressing, joyful cares attending this summon to herself" (431). This is exactly the situation in which the novel ends—with the whole Bertram family half-wrecked and Fanny Price returning to Mansfield Park with flying colors. The narrator notes in a patronizing, mocking tone: "My Fanny indeed at this very time, I have the satisfaction of knowing, must have been happy in spite of every thing. She must have been a happy creature in spite of all that she felt or thought she felt, for the distress of those around her" (446).

Fanny's double response is an internalized Crawford-Bertram dialogue and something more. As I mentioned before, her sense of what "should be"—dutiful gratitude to her uncle and tender consideration for all her relatives—is expressed by the Edmundian, orthodox language. It functions as a kind of a second thought, a rational censorship exerted on the more spontaneous first sensations. The self-reproaches formulated in the terms such as "ungrateful," or "insensibility" remind us not only of Edmund's, or even Mrs. Norris's banal moral teachings, but also of Pamela's immaculate behavior. With Fanny, as with many cinder girls before her who had no name, family, or property to uphold them, to be consciously good is to turn misfortune into a kind of power or strong point.

Moreover, concepts of traditional Christian virtue have in a way helped to expand Fanny Price's understanding and compassion. During the episode of the playacting, Fanny, the bystander and prompter, has "looked and listened, not unamused to observe the selfishness which, more or less disguised, seemed to govern them all" (156). She witnesses the anguish of Julia who is piqued at her sister Maria's irresponsible behavior: "Fanny saw and pitied much of this in Julia; but there was no outward fellowship between them. Julia made no communication, and Fanny took no liberties. They were two solitary sufferers, or connected only by Fanny's consciousness" (183).

The highlighted difference between Julia and Fanny here is in every sense crucial. Fanny is almost the only seer in the whole novel—with perhaps the exception of Mary Crawford, who *can* see if she cares to—who has a consciousness large enough to embrace other people's suffering, notwithstanding her own moral judgment of the particular person. Consequently, she is the only one who is capable of a meaningful double response. Being positioned at the very fringe of the master group in the world of Mansfield Park—partly a master, partly a servant—and the constant victim of other people's selfish pursuits, she by necessity understands better the inevitable interdependence of human relationship in both its negative and its constructive aspects, and suspects very much the high-spirited egoism of Mary Crawford.[7] Fanny is, alone among all characters, positioned to see the wrongs of solipsism. Sadly, she realizes the solitariness of modern individuals locked in the consuming concern for themselves. In this sense, her moralistic second thought, her self-reproach, is neither hypocritic parroting of Edmund's words nor sheer self-repression. It does not erase her initial impulsive response, does not even challenge the primacy of personal emotions; but it does complicate this initial response, with a full awareness of the gap between her true feelings and the accepted moral code, between her own interest and that of others. This makes her a thoughtful and sophisticated "individualist," perhaps the most "modern" personality among Austen's women.

The critical opinions about Fanny, the usually reticent woman and the unappealing speaker, are very diversified. Gilbert and Gubar, though they fully recognize the self-division of the author, do not properly explore Fanny Price's inner complexity and classify her, a little overhastily, as the docile, conforming Snow White type (155, 163–165).[8] D. W. Harding, on the other hand, perceives in the Cinderella theme a "regulated hatred" (164, 173–175). Kingsley Amis regards Fanny as "a monster of complacency and pride . . . under a cloak of cringing self-abasement" (144) and feels disgusted. Nina Auerbach thinks that Fanny's disturbing quality "invoke[s] the monsters" challenging the conventional boundary of realistic novels (24) and celebrates her as an implicitly disruptive female figure. The multiplicity of interpretations at once highlights the distinctive theoretical and ideological backgrounds of the commentators and demonstrates the radical unfitness of the character to be categorized. Fanny Price is usually too submissive, too declaredly—through an uneasy voice, though—conforming to be a real diabolic threat to the existing order. Yet she is also too silently resentful and too uncomfortably self-concerned to be an "angel," or even a naively complacent Pamela. On the whole, I think, in line with Nina Auerbach, that Fanny with her "power to offend" (Trilling 127) is closer to a perplexing "monster." It is not unlike the case of Jane Fairfax, the enigmatic true Cinderella in *Emma*. Though Jane's reticence gives her the appearance of meekness and humbleness, which is approved by all who feel socially superior to her, it actually hatches secret passions, discontents, and a self-fulfilling "plot." When Mr. Knightley says that she "has not the open temper which a man would wish for in a wife"(289), he obviously senses some danger and a threat in such feminine taciturnity.

The same can be said about Fanny Price. Silence, though originally imposed upon her by her humble position in the household, has increasingly become her conscious choice. When she is urged by all to take a part in the private theatricals, she pitifully pleads: " 'It is not that I am afraid of learning by heart,' said Fanny, shocked to find herself at that moment the only speaker in the room, and to feel that almost every eye was upon her: 'but I really cannot act' " (169). To act is to speak in another's voice, which Fanny has been doing all along and rather dislikes. Hence her preferred silence and her declaration, " 'I really cannot act,' " are no less than an attempted refusal of the prevailing discourses that are being forced upon her. For Fanny, language always falsifies her heart and mind and exposes her to the attacks from outside; silence is her protection and her puzzling fascination.

As the silent audience outside the social and erotic melodrama around her, Fanny gains the power of the prompter/spectator, like the power she possesses during the theatricals, when she knows everyone's lines and is the confidante of most of those self-serving performers. In the very ambiguous role of "prompter," Fanny places herself both inside and outside the theatrical activity, both speaks and keeps silent, both morally against acting and in a way secretly relishing it. If she is unable truly to control or command like an author or director, she can at least shield herself from harm with the knowledge gained through her unique speechless position.

When Jane Austen decided upon a "complete change of subject," she was also meditating on a shift in style: "I had some fits of disgust. . . . The work [*Pride and Prejudice*] is rather too light, and bright, and sparkling, it wants shade" (Chapman, *Austen's Letters* 298–299). Although she seems to be talking about pure stylistic problems, the gravely judgmental term "disgust" indicates perhaps something more is involved. The result of such deliberation is the rather "shady" *Mansfield Park*, in which the "light," "bright," and "sparkling" style is not only circumscribed by and contrasted with Fanny's persistent awkwardness and stubborn silence, but severely criticized and partially negated through the figure of its representative, Mary Crawford. Considering Austen's partiality for sprightly Elizabeth Bennet and her fondness for the "delicious play of Mind" (Chapman, *Austen's Letters* 478–479), she seems to be oddly stern in permanently exiling Mary's "lively mind" (95) from Mansfield Park. A second thought, however, would tell us that the author's reservations about such style are already amply manifested in *Pride and Prejudice*. Elizabeth is not "rewarded" with the happy marriage until she comes to view her father's flippant humor with a critical eye and has undergone some speechless moments of embarrassment.[9] And she is much luckier than Mary Crawford in being originally "blessed" with some occasional thoughtful silences.

A similar inference can be drawn from a comparison of Emma and Miss Fairfax. As a contrast to Emma Woodhouse,

the clever and outspoken "queen" of Highbury society, Jane
Fairfax, who is exactly the same age as Emma, is the self-conscious, poor orphan prepared for self-supporting work. She is
always, in Emma's critical eye, "wrapt up in a cloak of polite-
ness," and "suspiciously reserved" (182). With no little irritation, Emma complains that she could not squeeze from Jane
any true opinion about young Churchill:

> "Was he handsome?"—"She believed he was reckoned a very
> fine young man." "Was he agreeable?"—"He was generally
> thought so." "Did he appear a sensible young man; a young
> man of information?"—"At a watering-place, or in a common
> London acquaintance, it was difficult to decide on such points.
> Manners were all that could be safely judged of. . . . She be-
> lieved every body found his manners pleasing." (182–183)

Emma, with her usual sharpness, wonderfully catches Jane's way
of speaking without saying. Miss Fairfax is certainly a consum-
mate master in more skills than just piano-playing. Fearing to ex-
pose her secret engagement with Frank, and entertaining some
reasonable doubt about his character, Jane prudently adopts the
safe strategy of repeating others' words. However, much more
mature and critical-minded than Fanny Price, she watchfully dis-
engages herself from public opinion and other "copied" languages. Her peculiar way of speaking accomplishes the
remarkable act of double "un-saying." On one level, she erases
her own utterances by deliberately highlighting their sources—
"He is *generally* thought so," "*every body* found him pleasing"
(my emphasis)—and thereby reinforces the fact that *she* is not expressing any opinion on the subject. At the same time, Jane's evasive speeches, which obstinately exclude herself from the cited
"every body" imply a critique of, even an effective negation of,
those public opinions themselves. Moreover, the narrative offers
evidence that when she chooses to, Jane wants neither the courage and skill to divulge her mind, as when she speaks to Mrs.
Elton about "the sale . . . of human intellect" (300) with suppressed bitterness; nor the passion and determination to reach a
decision—as she rashly "strikes" her engagement or resolutely

accepts a job offer. If it is the authorial intention to shake and shatter the false sense of social and intellectual security and superiority that have nourished Emma's ready tongue and tempted her to pretend to be a "godmother" to Harriet, and to bring Emma down to her true status—not exactly a Cinderella, but nevertheless a less secure, motherless girl who is only too happy to embrace the average power and happiness of espousing a true gentleman; then it must be noted that the same author is unusually "lenient" toward Jane, the out-of-focus, reluctant double talker. Jane, who is supposed to have learned her lesson before the story opens, not only has her Cinderellean plan built on an "imprudent" passion come true, but also reserves, uniquely among all Austen's marriageable young girls, the potential to be an independent working woman.

The critics who deem the lively, ironic tone of Emma and Elizabeth Bennet as being closest to the author's voice have intentionally or unintentionally overlooked the evidence supporting a different conclusion. The narrator in Austen's novels has at least two alternative voices. In nearly every book, the narrator at a decisive point in her heroine's development, turns from a condescending satirist/parodist into a sentimental storyteller. In *Persuasion*, the voice of the satirist nearly disappears. Austen, though a versed and graceful speaker in both narrative voices, is, like Fanny Price, not completely comfortable with either. That is why she shifts between the two, constantly commenting on one through the other.

Elizabeth Bennet finally achieves a happy, though precarious, balance between speech and silence.[10] But neither Mary Crawford nor Fanny Price manages to escape her linguistic dilemma. Fanny never gets over her fear and uneasiness about speaking, and, most significantly, leaves the truth about her long love for Edmund unspoken even at the end. In her very unloveliness, Fanny seems to tell, more than anything else, the mental toll exacted by living in her assigned role of a bourgeois Cinderella. And Mary is still trapped in frivolous jokes when we last hear about her. In *Mansfield Park*, language somehow belies and betrays every woman.[11] Though Mary's comment on Maria Rushworth's elopement with her brother—"what can equal the folly of our two relations?"—sounds light and heartless and has "shocked" Edmund (440–441), she might actually be as annoyed as Edmund would want her to be. That she applies "no harsher name than folly" (441) is due to the fact, in all likelihood, that "folly" *is* the usual "harsh" reproach in the vocabulary she has adopted from the London social circle around her. In Jane Austen's world, not even Mary, for all her money, wit, and beauty (which have spoiled her), can speak freely and with complete immunity. After all, she belongs to the sex to be judged and regulated, and her "immoral" joke about the Henry-Maria elopement is the last straw. Edmund, the gentleman/hero, finally becomes disgusted with her. The author here seems to be presenting the linguistic poverty of women as the second sex. In *Persuasion* another quiet heroine overtly comments on the gender bias of language and literature: "Men have had every advantage of us in telling their own story. Education has been theirs in so much higher a degree; the pen has been in their hand. I will not allow books to prove any thing" (237).

To make speechlessness the subject of language is self-problematizing, if not impossible. By ostracizing talkative Mary and Mrs. Norris and by making Fanny upsettingly silent, Austen implicitly raises questions and doubts about her own enterprise—that of telling a story with a plot and languages inherited from the *others*.

At the end of the novel, Sir Thomas, who is originally most worried about "cousins in love" (43), willingly gives his hearty welcome to Fanny as a daughter-in-law. The narrator then comments on how "the plans and decisions of mortals" (455) are to be contradicted or revised by time and actuality.

As far as Fanny is concerned, there are three leading "plots," which parallel and fight each other. The first is Mrs. Norris's plan to have her brought up in Mansfield Park, which is propelled by her desire to display her "kindness" as well as to heighten her own social position by keeping someone beneath herself. "The trouble and expense of it . . . would be nothing

compared with the benevolence of the action," says she persuasively to her sister, Lady Bertram, "lobbying" for Fanny's case.
Her speech to Sir Thomas, who is still hesitating, sounds even
more pompously "heroic" and self-celebrating: "Do not let us
be frightened from a good deed by a trifle. . . . A niece of *our's*,
Sir Thomas, I may say, or, at least of *your's*, would not grow
up in this neighbourhood without many advantages" (43–44,
my emphasis). The subtle shift in her speech between "our's"
and "your's" reveals Mrs. Norris's wish to raise herself to the
status of a Bertram through this joint project of charity, and
her constant abusing, scolding, and lecturing of the girl further
bears out this intention. In a way she is indeed a plot-maker and
a malicious stepmother figure. But what needs to be added is
that her plot—i.e., to make Fanny living proof of the social
and moral superiority of the Bertrams and herself—is the plot
endorsed by the elder Bertrams when they accept their poor
niece into their house. In other words, Mrs. Norris's plot is a
patriarchal one, though she herself is but another dependent female relation wanting to share the heeltap of the power and
glory of Mansfield Park.

However, Fanny does not mean to be a humble dependent
forever, and that is why she strenuously endeavors to secure
her only friend, Edmund. It is hard to decide exactly when her
sisterly attachment to Edmund matures into a conscious marriage plot—perhaps by the time Edmund neglects her riding
exercise for Mary Crawford's sake and provokes in her the first
actual pain. The "forces" that Fanny gathers to confront Mary's
heavy offensive are, like those of Tolstoy's famous Russian
commander before Napoleon, "patience and time" (885). She
retreats and holds her tongue until the invading Crawfords have
managed to defeat themselves, as well as largely to demolish
the Mansfield Park order. Then she happily comes forth, successfully marries her chosen man, and becomes the spiritual
mainstay in reconstructing Mansfield Park. She triumphs over
the Bertrams by becoming a Bertram. Whether it is a double
victory, a victory in defeat, or a defeat in victory—or all the
three—is up to the reader to decide.

Although Fanny's plot proves to be the only one subscribed

to by the narrative "providence," somehow this Cinderella lacks the glamour that is necessary for her romantic destiny. In the original fairy tale, some of the details are very physical, and, implicitly, very erotic: the splendid ball, the intoxicating dance, the tiny glass slipper. Yet little personal attraction, physical or stylistic, is assigned to Fanny Price. As Nina Auerbach points out, there is the intriguing absence of love in the hero for the heroine (30–33). While Fanny is too insecure to proclaim her love, Edmund is extraordinarily obtuse about her feelings. Even when the novel is drawing to its end, this irresolute young man is still confessing to Fanny that Mary is "the only woman in the world whom I could ever think of as a wife" (412), and, to Fanny's great pain, elaborates on what steps he would take to win that lady. If any actual "courtship" between Edmund and Fanny is ever touched upon at all, it is treated in a light, playful, and condescending way, more to brush it aside than to draw any attention to it:

> Edmund had greatly the advantage of her [Mary Craw-ford] in this respect. He had not to wait and wish with vacant affections for an object worthy to succeed her in them. Scarcely had he done regretting Mary Crawford, and observing to Fanny how impossible it was that he should ever meet with such another woman, before it began to strike him whether a very different kind of woman might not do just as well—or a great deal better; whether Fanny herself were not growing as dear, as important to him in all her smiles, and all her ways, as Mary Crawford had ever been; and whether it might not be a possible, an hopeful undertaking to persuade her that her warm and sisterly regard for him would be foun-dation enough for wedded love.
>
> I purposely abstain from dates on this occasion, that every one may be at liberty to fix their own, aware that cure of unconquerable passions, and the transfer of unchanging at-tachments, must vary much as to time in different people.— I only intreat every body to believe that exactly at the time when it was quite natural that it should be so, and not a week earlier, Edmund did cease to care about Miss Crawford, and

became as anxious to marry Fanny, as Fanny herself could desire. (454)

Apparently there is little passion on Edmund's part, no matter how much he is convinced of the advisability of marrying his quiet cousin. No wonder that even after the desired marriage is enacted, cool-minded Fanny is still cautious and silent, and dares not to indulge one little whim. Their marriage, being somewhat "incestuous," and "a turning inward toward the family rather than embrace of new connections which traditionally comes at the affirmative end of comedies" (Brownstein 112), is in a way dampening and claustrophobic, almost an anticlimax.[12]

The third "plot" concerning Fanny is that of Henry Crawford. His is the scheme of a typical rake; as he once pronounces to his sister Mary, "my plan is to make Fanny Price in love with me" (239). Like Mr. B, Sir Clement Willoughby, and all the artful seducers indispensable for the narrative pattern, he functions as the moral touchstone for the true heroine. The charming tempter is designed, as D. W. Harding says, to be "resisted by the morally perceptive Cinderella" ("Introduction" to Penguin *Persuasion* 24). That is to say, Henry's failure is decreed by the convention. Even his fascination with Fanny's opposition and his half-hearted determination for reformation are well within the variation of the same plot—following the footsteps of that seasonably amended Mr. B. Although this willful young man, who suddenly assumes the role of serious lover and responsible landlord, finds himself trapped again in a casual flirtation in the last chapter, when all the loose ends are being wound up, the narrative at least for a moment reflects on the likelihood of another conclusion:

Could he [Henry Crawford] have been satisfied with the conquest of one amiable woman's affections, could he have found sufficient exultation in overcoming the reluctance, in working himself into the esteem and tenderness of Fanny Price, there would have been every probability of success and felicity for him. . . . Would he have persevered, and up-rightly, Fanny must have been his reward—and a reward very voluntarily bestowed—within a reasonable period from Edmund's marrying Mary. (451)

This alternative narrative, though making no great difference for the ruling pattern of the Cinderella-like rise of the heroine, would make the ending considerably more cheerful, more in the spirit of a true romantic comedy, and the book would be much less a "problem" novel.[13] It would suggest that Fanny is, after all, being loved wholeheartedly and passionately by her prince and would allow the fairy tale pattern to be adequately fulfilled. Yet this possibility, only mentioned in the subjunctive mood, is denied in the "actual" life of the character. Fanny is destined to be the oddly unloved heroine of a love story.

In the final analysis, Fanny's troublesome relationship with her designated role in the genre, or rather, the subgenre of the perse-cuted young woman's love story, is perhaps the cause of our var-ious discomforts about her. Nearly every woman in the novel thinks in terms of the "duty" of marrying advantageously, which is a vulgarized and debased version of the same Cinderella plot that has governed the heroine's lot.[14] It appears as if the au-thor wants Fanny Price to redeem the true Pamela tradition from those "corrupted" forms. The result is a most perplexed and per-plexing heroine. As the paragon to be rewarded for her merits, she loses Pamela's single-minded moral complacency and feels rather awkward at using the language of the social and ethical conventions; as the heroine who is going to get her heart's desire, she is always ambivalent about her own genuine feelings; as the cinder girl who finally marries successfully, she is strangely de-prived of the love of a prince. And her path to new social heights and marital felicity is too close to the plot of advantageous mar-riage contemplated by Maria Bertram and Mary Crawford to es-cape the criticism aimed at the latter. Whatever we name such self-conflicting elements—call it "ironic twist" or "realistic re-writing"—the romantic love story that is contained in the novel and is essentially *the novel* is very much "cramped" and damaged.

In her novels, Austen often eventually reaffirms what she apparently sets out to deride at the beginning. Catherine Morland's education consists largely of Henry Tilney's mocking her girlish reading of Gothic romances; yet all her daydreams and her interpretations of life that are based on such readings are supported by the unfolding of the plot. The famous beginning of *Pride and Prejudice* opens with an ironical recapitulation of the dearest scheme of Mrs. Bennet: "It is a truth universally acknowledged, that a single man in possession of a good fortune must be in want of a wife" (51). But the brilliant marriage contract that her smart Elizabeth strikes in the end outshines Mrs. Bennet's wildest plotting. Perhaps the old convention, however abused and deteriorated, still contains too much truth, literarily and literally, to be completely dispensed with. Perhaps in the old Cinderella story there is still space for a heroine to work out her self-fulfillment, no matter how qualified. Yet, in spite of the author's overt intention to offer in *Mansfield Park* an authentic, truly worthy Cinderella in contrast with those false, self-indulgent ones, what we have is an embodiment of far-reaching doubt and perplexity toward the narrative pattern and the languages that weaved it.

CHAPTER FOUR

Charlotte Brontë: Toward the New Plot

> It seems that even "a lone woman" can be happy, as well as cherished wives and proud mothers—I am glad of that—I speculate much on the existence of unmarried and never-to-be-married women nowadays, and I have already got to the point of considering that there is no more respectable character on this earth than an unmarried woman who makes her own way through life quietly, perseveringly—without support of husband or brother. . . .
>
> —Charlotte Brontë

Jane Eyre is but another Pamela, Elizabeth Rigby said in a rather disparaging tone more than one hundred years ago (106). Though most of her deprecations of Charlotte Brontë's first published novel are simply forgotten now, the similarity she noticed between Jane Eyre and Richardson's class-climbing maid has been observed by readers again and again.[1] Many critics further attribute their characterization to their common "ancestor"—that ever-envied and ever-imitated Cinderella. Karen E. Rowe points out: "Jane Eyre outwardly resembles classic fairy tale heroines, as critics often acknowledge by likening her progress to Cinderella's ascent from hearth to palace" (" 'Fairyborn' " 72). To support this statement, she gives an impressive list of relevant critical works, ranging from Richard Chase's "The Brontës, or Myth Domesticated" to Helene Moglen's *Charlotte Brontë: The Self Conceived* (328).

The narrator/heroine in *Jane Eyre* is very conscious of this fairy tale pattern. The opening scene of the novel forms a manifest analogy to the situation of Cinderella's family. While the Reed children gather by the fireside around their indulgent mother, Jane Eyre alone is excluded and banished to a window seat (*window* again!); she is reading a book about birds, which is for young Jane "as interesting as the tales Bessie sometimes narrated on winter evenings" (9). Indeed, Bessie the nurse seems to be Jane's chief mentor; she has fed the children's "eager attention with passages of love and adventure taken from old fairy tales and older ballads; or . . . from the pages of Pamela, and Henry, Earl of Moreland" (9). For girls barred from formal education like Jane, folk tales and oral literature are the *Iliad* and *Odyssey* that cast their perception and imagination. Consequently, Jane Eyre, being the frightened child shut up in the "Red Room," views her own reflection in the glass as "half fairy, half imp" (14); and even as an adult, she still thinks of her life in terms of a fairy tale situation and compares the third floor of Thornfield to the "corridor in some Bluebeard's castle" (108).

Directly related to Jane's classical Cinderellean position in the family is her frantic rebelliousness. Talking about her exclusion from the fireside, the narrator says with accentuation: "Me, she [Mrs. Reed] had dispensed from joining the group" (7). Be it an accurate recording of a child's bitterness, or a more detached presentation of the episode by the older Jane looking back, the inverted word order of the sentence points to the distressing discrepancy between the subjective and the objective worlds. In the former, this *me*, which is moved to the forefront and boldly assumes the place of a *subject*, an *actor*, is obviously the number-one figure; in the latter it remains—as it is in the actual syntax—an object, a thing to be acted upon.

As a middle-class cinder girl, young Jane Eyre has a history that stretches back more than one hundred years. The long struggles of various of Pamela's daughters, and the painful self-reflections accompanying them, enable this new heroine to see her situation more clearly and honestly. She knows she is deprived and degraded, and wrongly. Not merely harboring a secret wish for change like a typical fairy tale heroine, Jane, the heiress of the Romantics, openly speaks out against abuse and oppression. She loudly calls her bullying cousin John Reed a "slave-driver" and a "murderer" (11), and literally fights back with her hands and body in a way that would shock fine ladies like Evelina. With Jane Eyre, the dynamic dissatisfaction and disobedience, which are inevitable for every Cinderella exiled to the window position, surface in the narrative and are openly acknowledged by the heroine herself. Her mutinous spirit, though a far cry from female propriety, is nevertheless closely related to the maneuvering of ladies like Evelina toward earthly felicity. It is this intense anger, which is the expression of her thwarted romantic expectations, that moves Jane away from Gateshead and into the adventure of her life.

If the beginning has posited little Jane as the typical persecuted "innocent" and a ferocious rebel against the hierarchy of the Gateshead house, the further unfolding of her "autobiography" demonstrates that the grown-up Jane is both a tenacious romantic aspirer and a serious questioner of that age-old Cinderella dream. Factors that curb and revise the fairy tale spirit are touched upon even in the early chapters. The brief mention of the texts about Pamela or the popular version of the history of Henry, Earl of Moreland, by John Wesley is enough to suggest the powerful Christian moral tradition that is woven into the oral literature that constitutes Jane's elementary education. Bessie's ballad, beginning with

My feet they are sore, and my limbs they are weary
   Long is the way, and the mountains are wild;
Soon will the twilight close moonless and dreary
   Over the path of the poor orphan child. (22)

focuses on the themes of suffering and death. With the ending note, "Heaven is a home," and the emphasis on the Bunyanesque image of a "journey," the ballad tries to give suffering a meaning—not as the prelude to worldly glory and pleasure, as in case of Cinderella, but as an arduous pilgrimage to God and hence glory in itself.[2] The psychological swing between the two poles—the romantic aspiration for love and self-realization and a strained asceticism, partly religious and partly secular, that holds a rather bleak, "realistic" view of life—becomes a kind of motivating force that drives the heroine and her story forward.

For a closer look at Jane's emotional seesawing, we may compare two of her internal monologues. One occurs at the end of her Lowood school experience of self-discipline and forbearance:

> I tired of the routine of eight years in one afternoon. I desired liberty; for liberty I gasped; for liberty I uttered a prayer; it seemed scattered on the wind then faintly blowing. I abandoned it, and framed a humbler supplication; for change, stimulus: that petition, too, seemed swept off into vague space; "Then," I cried, half desperate, "Grant me at least a new servitude!" (86)

The other turns up after Jane's encounter with Rochester at Thornfield, when she tries desperately to suppress her own unseemly attraction to her master:

> "Could not even self-interest make you wiser? . . . It does good to no woman to be flattered by her superior, who cannot possibly intend to marry her; and it is madness to all women to let a secret love kindle within them, which, if unreturned and unknown, must devour the life that feeds it; and if discovered and responded to, must lead, *ignis fatuus*-like, into miry wilds whence there is no extrication." (163)

The second passage on "self-interest," with its distanced, second-person arguments and the generalized, third-person rationalizations, sounds very familiar. It reminds us of many of the amazingly sensible reasonings voiced by heroines like Pamela or Emmeline. What is more strikingly Jane-Eyrean is the breathless, emotional style of the first passage. Each of the three sentences in this passage opens with "I," and the verbs used ("tired," "desired," etc.) are direct, unequivocal, and forceful. Conspicuously, there are frequent "gasping" stops within the limit of these relatively short sentences. A comma or a semicolon often interrupts after two or three words, as if the silent speaker literally pants for breath. Such breathlessness points at once to the insufferable oppressiveness of her Lowood life and to the "stirring of old emotions" (85) of that passionate little rebel at the beginning of the novel. Clearly present in that passage is a boiling, romantic longing. Though nothing about "love" is mentioned, the sexual drive and the libidinal energy underlying such excited'monologues are too self-evident to be mistaken. In the world of romantic love, a young girl's longing for new places and new faces, like Cinderella's wish to go to the ball, is never completely without a Prince Charming somewhere in mind. Through the maddening passion conveyed in this passage, the personal romantic impulse of the heroine is being brought to a new pitch and a new intensity, bordering on open social protest and rebellion.

Debating with herself, Jane collects into her armory the values of the romantic generation, such as "nature," "impulse," "feeling." Sometimes she switches to the other side of the argument as soon as she finishes admonishing herself about unwise passion. She vehemently revolts against the tyranny of reason and modesty and denounces her own rational thinking and attempted self-control as "blasphemy against nature" (177). Unlike a demure Evelina, Jane is strong enough to be candid with herself: instead of hiding the true nature of her "regards" toward her master, she insists with ardor and dignity on her right to love and the righteousness of such feelings.

These dialogues with herself go on and on. During the time when she is supposedly "engaged" to Rochester, Jane, the bride-to-be, at once eagerly looks forward to the all-important wedding with which most Cinderella stories reach their happy conclusion, and yet remains clear-headed enough to cautiously collect and decode all kinds of signs about her future lot. In her eyes, the smile of Rochester, who now tries to load her with jewelry and fine clothes, is "such as a sultan might, in a blissful and fond moment, bestow on a slave his gold and gems had enriched." She is disturbed by "a sense of annoyance and degradation" (271–273). Throughout the novel, Brontë uses "slave" as a metaphor to define the situation of a propertyless woman; therefore, it is not suprising that Jane finds Rochester's sultanlike smile so disturbing. Half-playfully, but nevertheless half-earnestly, she introduces the topic of "mutiny" and the "charter" to be forced upon the husband/despot. She negotiates with him about the payment for her future domestic labor (i.e., to continue working as Adele's "governess"). "I will not be your English Celine Varens [Rochester's French mistress]" (272), she declares, never forgetting the stories of those "poor girls" that Rochester has told her. Obviously, the fear that constantly haunts Jane is not only that the intended marriage might not come true, but also that it will come true and turn into a nightmare.

Much has been said about Jane's encounter with Mrs. Bertha Rochester, the sudden disclosure of whose existence wrecks Jane's marriage plot. Some critics have persuasively demonstrated that murderous Bertha, in her mad hatred and vengefulness, incarnates Jane Eyre's repressed, unconscious anger against her male master (Eagleton, *Myths of Power* 32; Gilbert and Gubar 356–362). The immured woman in Rochester's house can also be taken as the Victorian secret of sexuality carefully kept from young girls (Moglen 125–127). However, Bertha, Rochester's Creole wife from the West Indies, is more than an embodiment of some psychological and personal reality. She is, or at least in the novel's framework she is supposed to be, a social fact. Her very existence is a condemnation of the marriage glorified by the Victorians as the private paradise, a configuration of the scandalous, ugly history involving upper-class familial betrayal and warfare caused by patrimony, utterly mercenary marriage, British colonialist activities, which is suppressed by her male master. No matter how willingly Jane believes in Edward Rochester's version of their shared past, she somehow intuits that there is another side of the coin, in which the degraded and degrading madwoman Bertha is more the victim than the villain. This is the reason that she takes Rochester's rhetorical question literally: when he asks her, "If you were mad, do you think I should hate you?" she firmly answers: "I do indeed, sir" (305).

This is a turning point in the development of the narrative. Up to this moment, Jane's "desire" and "reason" have collaborated with each other, working toward a Cinderella-like finale. Now her anguished internal dialogue struggles to find a different resolution. For the first time, her usually defensive reason forces her into *action*—to flee the familiar snare of the old romantic plot and move out into new, uncharted waters. Having fled Thornfield and Rochester, Jane undergoes a series of tri-als—starvation, humiliation, and a long, deadly faint. Finally she wakes up into a new family, the Riverses, much as though she has gone through a symbolic rebirth. With two sisters and a cousin/brother named John, this new family exactly resembles the Reeds.[3] But here she is loved and valued: instead of being a penniless foundling, she is metamorphosed into an heiress and a benefactress, who brings fresh money and fresh love into the family.

Thus we can see that what happens after the aborted marriage is a kind of rewriting of the earlier part of the novel. For the readers who view Jane's life as a continuous personal "prog-ress," this separation of the lovers is the final stage of their moral development that enables the final reunion (Qualls 60–69; Showalter 112–122). However, if we read the novel as an exploration of a woman's plot, we will find the post-Thornfield part not only a revision of what happens before, but a continua-tion of the free play of mind begun in the "Angria" tales. A curious feature about this group of stories is that, while the male protagonist (Arthur Wellesley/Duke of Zamorna) remains basi-cally the same Byronic hero, the heroines who succeed one an-other differ vastly, and each story is named after one of them. Nearly every woman in that fantasy land of Angria—from the innocent, gentle Marian, to the passionate yet agonized wife Mary, to the unconditionally devoted mistress Mina—is with-out exception madly in love with *the hero,* and without excep-tion tormented and heartbroken. It is as if young Charlotte is testing with these fictional types woman's possible fate in rela-tion to man. Interestingly, it is not until she produces a new "amalgam" in a woman named Elizabeth Hastings, who, living on her teaching job, is "dependent on nobody, responsible to nobody," and "as prosperous as any little woman of five feet high and not twenty years old need wish to be" (Beer 351–352) that Charlotte willingly bids farewell to "Angria."

Jane Eyre moves this literary experiment into the more recog-nizable social context of early-nineteenth-century English life. In Jane's decision to leave Thornfield, two of the Angrian choices are definitely turned down, Mary's and Mina's. For all the fervent love Rochester has displayed, Jane is mature enough to guard against the lot of being a slave-wife or a blindly obedient mistress. From the perspective of the Angrian tales, Jane's "deserting" Rochester is predetermined long before the character comes into being.

More notably, Jane refuses two other "projects" for her life during her stay with the Riverses. One of these choices appears to be similar to that of Elizabeth Hastings', that is, to take teaching as a serious career. Once Jane pronounces that teaching is her *only* plan: "The utmost I hope is, to save money enough out of my earning to set up a school some day in a little house rented by myself" (200). But she feels distressed and degraded when she does get an unpretentious school for children of poor peasants, with a salary of thirty pounds a year, which is exactly the sum she asks from Rochester for taking care of Adele after their marriage. "I doubted I had taken a step which *sank instead of raising me in the scale of social existence*," says Jane to herself (363, my emphasis), not at all embarrassed by her own social snobbishness. Her distant attitude, if not contempt, toward the uncultivated poor people forms a sharp contrast to her clinging attachment to the genteel Riverses, who are regarded by Jane as her own "kind," even before their kinship is revealed. Elizabeth Hastings, the ideal "independent" woman of young Brontë, takes up work only to save enough money to "retire" as a "fine lady." The possibility of staying at the village school is quickly given up by Jane, because in this more realistic scene, teaching, instead of being the ladder to ascend to the social class of gentleman/lady, seems to promise only drudgery and emotional starvation.

Jane's rejection of St. John Rivers is more ambiguous and slippery in its implications. St. John's proposal is at once elevating and enslaving. He is the only person who hopes Jane would "look a little higher than domestic endearments and household joys" (395) and tries to recruit her as a Carlylean "fellow-labourer" (407). "What aim, what purpose, what ambition in life have you now?" he critically questions her (394). On the other hand, he is a kind of tyrant who ruthlessly imposes his will on her and intends to "own" her body and soul. He demands wifely submission from Jane without giving love: "I want a wife: the sole helpmeet I can influence efficiently, and retain absolutely till death" (411). Jane rightfully understands the worldly nature of his ambition when she compares him to "Christian or Pagan" heroes, lawgivers, statesmen, and conquerors. St. John is, in his own way, another fiery Romantic, though perhaps more Shelleyan than Byronic (Stone 118). Even his self-abnegation is fervent and frantic, rather than "cold," betraying a passion, or, more accurately, a conflict of oppositional passions.

For better or worse, Jane does not quite share St. John's ambition and adventurousness. "I have no vocation," she unequivocally answers him (407). The battle within her divided self now is less between a religious aspiration and a more humanistic longing for love, than between the impulse to yield and give up the burdensome responsibility of independence and the wish to stick to her own identity: "I was tempted to cease struggling with him—to rush down the torrent of his will into the gulf of his existence, and there lose my own" (423). It is only with the intervention of nature, or rather, the supernatural—which is an obvious manifestation of the narrative intention—that Jane manages to resist St. John with his forceful language of religion and heroic "project of soul-making" (Spivak 248). On the very point of surrender, she suddenly hears the voice of Rochester and therefore decides to set off on the trip back to her lover.

Ironically, what Jane has fought so hard to defend as her "own" will turns out to be nothing more than the common social role assigned to woman. She becomes a loving wife and mother, just as the moral preachment of the time taught women.[4] This paradox runs through the ending. On the one side we hear the assertive heroine's triumphant declaration: "Reader, *I* married him" (454, my emphasis), which calls to mind the abused yet defiant "me" at the beginning of the novel. The orphan girl, finally emerging from her prolonged spiritual journey, has transformed herself into a *subject,* an *actor.* In a sense Jane has almost "overreached" herself in her pursuit of equality—"Equal, as we are!" she announces during the eventful evening when she first desperately admits her love to Rochester (256)—for the impoverished and disabled Rochester is now less than an equal for the Jane Eyre with her newly found money and family. The sexual roles seem to have been inverted. Rochester, now sightless and mutilated, is "buried" in a small estate deep in the forest. It is Jane's role to break the baneful magic spell and bring her lover back to life. She teases and manipulates, arouses his jealousy and bestows little endearments in as overbearing a manner as he used to employ. In a word, the truant Cinderella now returns a little queen. She enters into a very different marriage in a quite different way.

Nevertheless, all these painstaking efforts to rewrite the Cinderella paradigm are quietly undercut by some short statements about the ten years of her happy married life:

> I hold myself extremely blest—blest beyond what language can express; because I am my husband's life as fully as he is mine. No woman was ever nearer to her mate than I am: ever more absolutely bone of his bone, and flesh of his flesh. . . .
>
> Mr. Rochester continued blind the first two years of our union: perhaps it was that circumstance that drew us so very near—that knit us so very close; for I was then his vision, as I am still his right hand. Literally, I was (what he often called me) the apple of his eye. (456)

The language here, with its overt and recurrent Biblical allusions, is conventional. So is the life it depicts. After all, Jane can only find happiness and a meaningful life through a man, by dissolving herself into his life. The readers who "repress or dismiss" Jane's Moor House experience and only care for the romantic marriage (Rowe, " 'Fairy-born' " 89), are doing so with a reason.[5] The marriage plot, after being questioned, interrupted, twisted, and distorted, finally reestablishes itself.

Many modern critics have noticed the limiting aspect of this compromised and compromising "solution." Neither Jane the narrator, nor Charlotte Brontë, is totally unconscious of it. She does not forget to add an "autumnal" (Martin 90) touch to Jane's matrimonial bliss. The Rochesters' new home—their earthly Eden—is a lonely and unhealthy place, to which Rochester's Victorian conscience has forbidden him to commit his mad wife Bertha. The Ferndean denouement is less a fulfillment

than imaginative exhaustion. In this light it is interesting that
the last word is given to St. John Rivers, who "is unmarried"
and "never will marry" (458). St. John, facing death, is desexualized: he is neither a man nor a woman, but a way of life outside the marriage plot. Now that he is no longer a threatening
male, Jane attempts to take another look at his life and spares
no high-flown verbal glorification. Rivers is compared to Bunyan's Greatheart and his namesake St. John. Together with the
Bunyanesque language used here, the "project of soul-making"
represented by St. John's missionary life is a cultural heritage
that Jane is born into, lives on, but nevertheless often fights
against—especially when its monastic stoicism conflicts with
her longing for emotional and sexual fulfillment. However
equivocal her attitude to St. John, the ending, which stresses
his choice of adventure, hardship, and "noble" work, forms a
comment on Jane's closed domestic life. It is like adding to the
end of the Cinderella story a passage from *The Pilgrim's Progress*.
The two distinct narratives collide with each other.

Rochester, in the disguise of a gypsy fortuneteller, says to
Jane, "Your fortune is yet doubtful: when I examined your face,
one trait contradicted another." Jane Eyre's psychological conflict is perceived by this ruling-class male as the opposition between the eye, which is "soft and full of *feeling*," and the
forehead, which declares that "*Reason* sits firm and holds the
rein" (202–203, myemphasis); his analysis neatly accords with
the familiar cultural dichotomy of passion and reason.[6]

Notably, in his definition of Jane's mental schism, Rochester
leaves out a crucial term of Jane's—"the real," which does not
quite fit into his binary system. The banner Jane raises against
her own romantic longing is neither the long-celebrated virtue
of modesty, nor the Helen Burns–like absolute self-abnegation,
but what Terry Eagleton calls "blunt bourgeois rationality"
(*Myths of Power* 4)[7]—namely, "common sense," "reason,"
"self-interest," and most significantly, "the real." She says:

> I . . . looked into my heart, examined its thoughts and feel-
> ings, and endeavoured to bring back with a strict hand such

as had been straying through *imagination's* boundless and trackless waste, into the safe fold of *common sense.*

. . . *Reason* having come forward and told, in her own quiet way, a plain, unvarnished tale, showing how I had rejected *the real* and rabidly devoured *the ideal* . . . . (162, my emphasis)

Evidently it is the Emmelinesque businesswoman's instinct that is at work to check the passions and steer them into safer waters. What such rationality confronts is not love or the self-fulfilling impulse itself, but the false romantic dream entangled with it.

In this set of "anti-Romantic" values, "the real" is posited against "the ideal," which is a synonym for the frequently cited "fairy tale," "dream," "imagination," etc. The problem of "the real" seems to have a special urgency for these women writers: nearly every novelist discussed here is obsessed with it. Frances Burney pronounces in the preface to *Evelina* that her intention is "to draw characters from nature" and decries "the fantastic regions of Romance" (xiii–xiv). Her heroine, not unlike Jane Eyre, tries strenuously to keep dream and imagination at bay. Mrs. Smith laughs at the girlish daydreaming of popular novels. The term "real" itself has multiple implications. It is related both to a moral attitude, which is usually called "rational" or "practical," and to the literary tradition of faithful representation of the *actual*. However, neither implication of the word seems to fit its usage by these women writers, who are by no means especially scrupulous about the rules of "verisimilitude" or "probability" of "realistic" writing, and whose heroines are usually ruled by their unspoken emotions. Yet this self-contradiction does not in the least dampen their enthusiastic concern with "the real." "The real" here as the *female word* appears to be a code name for a *different* plot. It is, we may say, a war cry against a specific pre-text—the powerful Cinderella fantasy as the blueprint for female life in and out of the novel. Jane the character has voiced her disparagement of "the tales": "They generally run on the same theme—courtship; and promise to end in the same catastrophe—marriage. . . . Positively I don't care about it: it is nothing to me" (201).

As we have noticed before, the Cinderella story is very much a middle-class myth that romanticizes woman's "mission" in a bourgeois nuclear family. This effort to see beyond "the tale" suggests an acute consciousness of the "rupture" between the socially valorized myth and the lived experience of women, or, as Mary Poovey puts it, "between the placating promise formulated by a ruling group and the actual material rewards the majority has access to" (xiv). It does not matter that the "lived experience" of an Emmeline or a Jane Eyre is but another fictional "tale" that still owes a lot to the old narrative paradigm. The very endeavor at "the real," the continual attempt to retell the story, marks a significant alienation from the prevalent gender fiction.

In this sense Jane Eyre's journey from Gateshead to Ferndean, via Thornfield and Marsh End/Moor House, is a long search for the "truth" beyond "the tale"; it proves to be a double-edged critique on both "the dream," the false mythical promise, and on the actual life of deprivation and humiliation. Notably, it is the male character Rochester who openly and insistently compares Jane to an "imp" and a "fairy" and evokes the spirit of the fairy tale (123, 152, 270, 273); whereas Jane the grown-up woman often tries desperately to break the charm of such illusions and "sweet lies" (162, 201, 261, 281).

This fascination with "the real" indicates a growing criticism of "the dream" that contains and sustains both "passion" and "reason." *Jane Eyre*'s ending, which is viewed by many critics as a meaningful compromise between passion and reason, is actually less than satisfactory in the light of this unfulfilled search for a different plot. The fact that Brontë more energetically renews her endeavor to reach "the real" after *Jane Eyre* tells of her dissatisfaction with both Rochester's reading of Jane and the "solution" the novel offers. At the very beginning of *Shirley,* the narrator asks her reader to be prepared for "something *real,* cool and solid . . . something *unromantic* as Monday morning" (40, my emphasis). Later, in 1852, Charlotte reasserts her "realistic" principle in her preface to *The Professor*: "My hero should work his way through life as I had seen *real* living men work theirs" (xi, my emphasis). In *Villette* this concern with "the real" or "the truth" is more constant and predominant. When the new heroine Lucy Snowe confronts her own split personality, she defines it in similar terms of "fancy" and "reality": "I seemed to hold two lives,—the life of thought, and that of reality" (140).

This does not mean, of course, that Lucy is completely liberated from the old "double room" mental prison of passion/reason. On the contrary, she still oscillates between the two in a most intense and torturing way. Typically, she writes two answers to Dr. John's letter: one is passionate, desperate, but suppressed as soon as it is written; the other one, which is actually sent, is friendly, grateful, and proper. However, she is at the same time sick with both: the morbid passionate desire, the "full liberal impulse of Feeling" that feeds on "dream" and can find no outlet in life, and the "dry, stinting check of Reason" that forces her to give up or compromise her aspirations (334). Lucy's revulsion of the sacred eighteenth-century term "reason" is especially strong: "This hag, this Reason, would not let me look up, or smile, or hope; she could not rest unless I were altogether crushed, cowed, broken-in, and broken-down" (307).

In another place Lucy compares her internal conflict to a Biblical situation—the relationship between Sisera and Jael. "My Sisera," as she calls it, is her nameless longing and emotions. It is being knocked on the head by Jael, "the stern woman." However, the picture of the opposition is considerately complicated when two other elements are introduced: "the ideal" and "Heber":

> I did long, achingly, . . . for something to fetch me out of my present existence, and lead me upwards and onwards. This longing, and all of a similar kind, it was necessary to knock on the head; which I did, figuratively, after the manner of Jael to Sisera. . . . Unlike Sisera, they did not die: they were but transiently stunned. . . .
>
> . . . My Sisera lay quiet in the tent, slumbering; and if his pain ached through his slumbers, something like an angel—the Ideal—knelt near, dropping balm on the soothed temples,

holding before the sealed eyes a magic glass, of which the sweet, solemn visions were repeated in dreams. . . . Jael, the stern woman, sat apart, relenting somewhat over her captive; but more prone to dwell on the faithful expectation of Heber coming home. (176)

The figurative language here is very vague, ambiguous, and open to different interpretations. And, as all comparison is in a way elusive and misleading, the Biblical context or the gender difference of these figures might greatly entangle our tentative interpretation of the fable in the novel. Nevertheless, one thing is certain: the picture of psychological war suggested by Lucy is not bilateral, but somehow dyadic. It would not be far-fetched to read "Heber" as something that transcends the original Sisera-Jael opposition, something that will finally dispel the "visions" (the romantic dreams) that Sisera craves and Jael tolerates; something, in a word, very close to the desired and searched for "real."

If we were to draw a kind of diagram of the relationship of the conflicting elements mentioned here, it would be something like this:

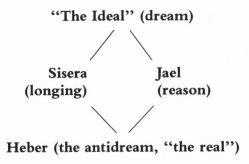

"The Ideal" (dream)

Sisera   **Jael**
(longing)   **(reason)**

Heber (the antidream, "the real")

Since in Brontë's texts "the ideal" and "the dream" are essentially what I named as the Cinderella theme (or the marriage plot), the extreme importance of this comparison of Lucy's to our subject is almost self-evident. There is, of course, no need to pin down the exact signified of these figures. What is most meaningful here is that this somewhat unwieldy fable suggests a vaguely intuited developmental pattern: through the continuous dialectic confrontations and negotiations between passion and reason, the old Cinderella paradigm is being blown open and something new and different is being attempted.

In *Villette,* the coexistence and contention of the cool-headed onlooker and the yearning cinder girl within the central character, Lucy Snowe, are crucial to the search for "the real." From the very beginning of her story, Lucy the narrator marginalizes herself and focuses the narrative spotlight on the highly emotional drama enacted by little Polly. By the time Polly Home comes to stay with Mrs. Bretton, Lucy's godmother, fourteen-year-old Lucy is already an alert observer and sign reader. When a few new pieces of furniture turn up in her room, she watchfully asks: "Of what are these things the signs and tokens?" (62). Mrs. Bretton tells Lucy not to pay too much attention to this sentimental new arriver, but she cannot help herself: "I did take notice: I watched Polly rest her small elbow on her small knee, her head on her hand; I observed her draw a square-inch or two of pocket handkerchief from the doll-pocket of her doll-skirt, and then I heard her weep" (65). The role of the decentralized spectator is as much forced upon Lucy by circumstance as self-chosen. She looks at Polly almost with the kind of self-conscious and professional interest with which a chemist watches his test tubes and bottles. She describes her looking as an "activity":

> It was curious to watch her as she washed and dressed, so small, busy, and noiseless. Evidently she was little accustomed to perform her own toilet; and the buttons, strings, hooks and eyes, offered difficulties which she encountered with a perseverance good to witness. She folded her night dress, she smoothed the drapery of her couch quite neatly; withdrawing into a corner . . . *I half rose, and advanced my*

head to see how she was occupied. On her knees, with her forehead bent on her hands, I *perceived* that she was praying. (66,
my emphasis)

At once amused and contemptuous, Lucy notices how the six-
year-old child nestles herself to her father; how this "little busy-
body" tries to serve her father at the table; how, after Mr.
Home's short visit, she gradually attaches herself to another
male protector—the handsome, playful, and carefree young
Graham Bretton, adjusting herself to his topics and interest, and
ministering to him like a little wife. Lucy soon decides that
Polly is not "interesting" when Graham is not around and
therefore "ceased to watch her under such circumstances" (81).
She also finds out that the child, though innocent, is a born
actress, who never shows Mrs. Bretton "one glimpse of her
inner self" (90). Lucy eagerly seizes every chance to examine
the chemical reaction of human feelings. When the message
comes that Polly must leave to join her father, Lucy is so curious about Polly's response that she takes upon herself "to communicate" the news to the child.

Perhaps most readers, influenced by conventional narratives,
would after the three introductory chapters assume that Lucy is
no more than a storytelling Nelly Dean. However, to our surprise and "disappointment," the idiosyncratic Polly who has
charmed us totally disappears from Chapter Four on, and only
makes an unimpressive return rather late in the novel. *Villette*
turns out to be the story of that cold, almost faceless spectator—
Miss Lucy Snowe. This betrayal of our expectations and the
departure from the familiar heroine type lead to a main theme
of the novel—the contrast and contradiction between the sentimental dependent woman and the steady, cynical bystander.
We can easily locate in that miniature lady, Polly Home, a can-
didate for a romantic heroine; but the sphinxlike watcher, Lucy,
is a new kind of woman in fiction, whose functions and implications are not so readily understood.

The characterization of the grown-up Lucy continues to
underline her "spectatorship." The young gazer grows into a

more self-conscious "looker-on at life" (211). Being a woman, she stands no chance for any satisfying professional career. And, having no money, no beauty, no friends, and no family, she can hardly squeeze into the only field assigned to young girls— the field of husband hunting. Even in the not unkind eyes of Dr. John Graham, the obscure Lucy is no more noticeable than "unobtrusive articles of furniture" (162). Lucy is forced, as she herself says, to practice "self-reliance and exertion" (95) and to remain a spectating outsider. No wonder her narrative is full of the utterances and doings of other people—her late invalid mistress/friend Miss Marchmont; the flippant, volatile beauty Ginevra Fanshawe; the "short and stout" (134) school directress Madame Beck, and so on. During her voyage to the Continent, Miss Fanshawe's disarming frankness and her shallow, shameless egotism draw attention from Lucy. During the first night Lucy spends at Madame Beck's pensionnat in Villette, she witnesses how that lady steals into her room, quietly scrutinizes her and every article of her personal belongings. Alone in a strange institution and a strange country, Lucy is too tired and too insecure to be angry with such an outrageous violation of her privacy. Moreover, she is rather occupied with her own counterwatching and sign-reading speculation: "Of what nature were the conclusions deduced from this scrutiny? Were they favourable or otherwise? Vain question. Madame's face of stone . . . betrayed no response" (132).

It is amazing how often people in *Villette* spy on each other. In this puzzling book, "spying, viewing, observation, voyeurism are all central activities" (Lawrence 456). The three major watchers in the novel are Madame Beck, M. Paul Emanuel, and our Lucy Snowe.[8] Morbid or not, they are the "seers." Unlike her "close" friends—Mrs. Bretton and Dr. John—Madame Beck and Paul are among the few who rightly recognize the savage woman in Lucy. The three quickly become aware of their common traits. Paul reads Lucy's head and face carefully and is absolutely sure of the "rapport" between Lucy and himself (457); and Lucy is willing to admit that Beck and she "understood each other well" (383). All of them are lonesome, self-conscious, and, to a degree, stoical. Perhaps due to their solitary life, they have developed a relish for voyeurism.

However, their differences are by far more important here than their similarities. With their distinct ways of spying, Madame Beck and M. Paul form a foil and a contrast to Lucy, which helps to delineate the nature of her onlooking. For Madame Beck, "surveillance," or "espionage" (135) is a part of her system of governing the school: it is the means employed in her essentially impersonal, desexualized politics, and usually bears no premeditated malice toward the person. By comparison, Paul's prying is a personal action with a strong sexist overtone. "You need watching, and watching *over*" (my emphasis), he says to Lucy self-righteously:

> "and it is well for you that I see this, and do my best to discharge both duties. I watch you and others pretty closely, pretty constantly, nearer and oftener than you or they think. . . . That is a room I have hired, nominally for a study—virtually for a post of observation. There I sit and read for hours together: it is my way—my taste. My book is this garden; it contents are human nature—female human nature." (453)

Even given his Catholic upbringing and moral acquiescence to his "Jesuit's system" of spying, this celibate gentleman's appetite for peeping on women is amazing. He not only rents a room specially for this purpose, but also uses a telescope (455). What is more stunning is his single-minded self-justification. He openly acknowledges his frequent visits to Lucy's desk and speaks of voyeurism as his sacred duty. Yet, paradoxically, his brazen confession in a way redeems his weird behavior: in him, voyeurism is compounded by his healthier general curiosity about the other sex and his masculine, protective concern for the woman he watches over.

Different from Paul or Beck, Lucy simply goes through life with a perceptive eye. She does not employ any trick nor often has she any practical end. Being denied almost any kind of active life, she channels her energy and intelligence into spectating and speculating. For her, to see is to know, to understand, and finally, as the arrangement of the narrative demonstrates, to develop a novelistic imagination. In an inchoate way Lucy senses a mission in her watching. That is why she directs her eyes with willing attention to all sorts of "irrelevant" passing figures: a contentedly married former schoolmate accidentally flitting by her side; the upper-class fop De Hamal stepping through the art gallery; or even a never-to-be-seen-again stewardess on a ship. When she inwardly says "brava" for Madame Beck's successful crushing of her brief affection for Dr. John (171), or when she gloats with a sneer over the madame's futile schemes to uncover Dr. John's love affair: "Ha! Ha! madame, your crafty wits are on the wrong track" (188), Lucy is by no means applauding self-abnegation or celebrating her own "heart-poverty" (186). Rather, passages like these dramatize the motionless action of watching. The exultant tone indicates a genuine excitement of a keen-eyed spectator looking at the display of human nature in the tragicomedy of life, which makes her for the moment forget her own miseries.

Yet, deep inside, this spectating bystander is a yearning woman. When out of necessity she accepts Miss Marchmont's offer of a job, Lucy describes her position: "Two hot, close rooms thus became my world; and a crippled old woman, my mistress, my friend, my all" (97). Beneath these simple words ferment the emotions of a turbulent soul: tender gratitude toward her friend; insurgent bitterness against the narrow and imprisoning space allotted to her; and deep sadness about the bare and bleak "my all." After Marchmont's sudden death, Lucy, left in a forlorn state, sets out to begin a new life. She gets to London and wakes up there in the morning with fresh hope: "I had a sudden feeling as if I, who had never yet truly lived, were at last about to taste life: in that morning my soul grew as fast as Jonah's gourd" (108). Propelled by her desire to "taste life," Lucy goes abroad, luckily finds a job at Madame Beck's school, and temporarily settles down in the Continental city of Villette. Dragging herself through the rigid and stifling routine at the pensionnat under Madame's diligent "surveillance," Lucy is, like Jane Eyre, again tormented by her longing for fuller life and love. After she recognizes in Dr. John the old acquaintance of her childhood, she find herself dazzled by his indefinable golden-reddish hair that once again floats before her eyes. In spite of all her invocations to "Reason" (251), she becomes more and more addicted to John Graham's friendly care. A letter from him means to her life and death:

> I took my letter, trembling with sweet impatience; I broke its seal.
> "Will it be long—will it be short?" thought I, passing my hand across my eyes to dissipate the silvery dimness of a suave, south wind shower.
> It was long.
> "Will it be cool?—Will it be kind?"
> It was kind.
> To my checked, bridled, disciplined expectation, it seemed very kind; to my longing and famished thought it seemed, perhaps, kinder than it was. (324)

Later, when she thinks the letter is lost, she cries and searches, like a "grovelling groping maniac" (326). Her behavior is so wildly passionate that only the blinded and emotionally self-absorbed Dr. John, who beholds the scene, can be foolish, or cunning, enough to miss the message of Lucy's agonized love.

The inner schism of Lucy Snowe is not quite the old warfare between "reason" and "passion." In Lucy, unlike in the case of Dorothea Brooke, self-sacrifice or self-denial is never a real motivation. Her constant resort to the Bible or Bunyan, and her stoic rationalizations, are desperate strategies for survival. Upon closer examination, we find that at every crucial point in her life, when some faint possibilities glitter before her, Lucy is never "bridled" from reaching for love and happiness by self-restraint. Once, at least once, she unequivocally announces: "A new creed became mine—a belief in happiness" (334). The little adventuress who enjoys the bustling city of London or who embarks alone on a ship bound for a new country can hardly fit the image of a self-effacing woman. Nor is much encouragement needed to set her smoldering passion fully aflame: just a few kind words from John Graham can make her beside herself, and a pledge of *"true* friendship" (500) from Paul is enough to make her defy Madame Beck (580).

Lucy's psychological split occurs more between an urge to remain a truth-seeing outsider and the painful longing for a more active and more fulfilling life. The two impulses, though inherently at variance with each other, may not be mutually exclusive, if they are not both invested and warped by the inherited languages. Lucy's desire to be an objective observer is often yoked to the rational or religious discourses of self-repression—the language associated with the oppressive social environment that has from the first exiled her to the position of a spectator. On the other hand, her instinctive aspiration for happiness and fulfillment can only find expression in the age-old plot of romantic love—the only happy story available for a woman's imagination. Because of these complications, Lucy's internal conflict becomes an insolvable tangle and an impossible impasse: to remain a spectator seems to entail insufferable deprivation and the perpetuation of a dismal actuality; yet to indulge the dream of love implies falling back upon the old pattern of romance, which, as young Lucy's half-derogatory attitude toward Polly suggests, the clear-eyed onlooker in the heroine can neither trust, nor appreciate unconditionally.

Lucy's psychological predicament is in a way bypassed or partially transcended in the narrative through a widening gap between Lucy the narrator and Lucy the heroine. There is a dual development. In relation to the heroine, we see progress toward her regaining the focal place—she first appears as a mere spectator but ends as the sentimental lover waiting for her man to return home. In terms of the narrative voice there is a gradual distancing of the narrator from the heroine—at the end of the novel, the irreconcilable psychological dichotomy in Lucy culminates in the final divorce between the narrator and the character.[9]

My godmother lived in a handsome house in the clean and ancient town of Bretton. . . .

When I was a girl I went to Bretton about twice a year, and well I liked the visit. . . . (61)

Thus begins the first chapter, immediately diving deeply into the past. Here, without the authorial intrusions that frequently turn up in the later parts of the novel, there is a curious merging of the narrator and the character. The storyteller seems to have completely endorsed young Lucy's point of view, yet the sophisticated language and the cynical voice unmistakably point to a cool and worldly-wise grown-up speaker:

It *was* not a noisy, not a wordy scene: for that I *was* thankful; but it *was* a scene of feeling too brimful, and which, because the cup *did* not foam up high or furiously overflow, only *oppressed* one the more. On all occasions of vehement, unrestrained expansion, a sense of disdain or ridicule *comes* to the weary spectator's relief; whereas I *have ever felt* most burdensome that sort of sensibility which bends of its own will, a giant slave under the sway of good sense. (71, my emphasis)

In this passage the tenses of the verbs change most smoothly. No interruptive reflection, nor alternation in tone or in the expressed feelings call attention to the switch from the "I" in the first sentence, which is connected to "was," to the "I" generalizing human experience in the second sentence coordinated with the present tense. There is another similar example, which deals with Polly's homesickness: "I, Lucy Snowe, *plead* guiltless of that curse, an overheated and discursive imagination; but whenever, opening a room-door, I *found* her seated in a corner alone, her head in her pigmy hand, that room *seemed* to me not inhabited, but haunted" (69, my emphasis). Here again the tenses change within a sentence. With the verb "plead" it is really hard to know which Lucy is the implied pleader. Judging from the grammar, it should be the older one, but such an assertion best

suits the naive young girl: the older Lucy, who is going to narrate her stormy emotional history with its various "overheated," hysterical episodes, must know herself better. Such
little confusions between the two Lucys in the first few chapters
are significant, especially in light of their gradual "estrangement" later in the novel. It is not by accident that when Lucy
is presented as the pure observer, the narrator identifies with
her most. A spiritual alliance between the young observer and
the older storyteller as a seminal theme is here tentatively suggested.

After these prefatory chapters, the narrator self-consciously
omits eight years of Lucy's life and resumes her storytelling in
quite a different tone. Adult Lucy's voyage to Villette and her
subsequent life there are a personal battle for self-assertion and
self-recentralization. In this process, she gradually loses her
willingness and ability to be a cool spectator. The most notable
manifestation of this is perhaps the change in her attitude toward Paulina (grown-up Polly). When they were roommates at
the Brettons, their relationship was not too cordial or warm.
We are told that before Polly's arrival, Lucy "was a good deal
taken notice of by Mrs Bretton" (61). In this small domestic
domain Lucy is literally displaced by Polly, the younger,
quainter, and more outgoing girl. Nevertheless, Lucy accepts
her dim new place without much fuss, treating Polly with
decent friendliness or even sincere sisterly compassion, and,
most importantly, standing aside and watching with interest
and pleasure. Years later, when Paulina, in the shape of a perfect
little countess, once again steals Dr. John's attention from Lucy,
Lucy is painfully hurt. She flatly refuses the better-paying job as
Paulina's companion and indignantly declares "I was no bright
lady's shadow" (382). It is her injured feelings, more than her
independence and self-respect, that Lucy is defending—after all,
she had once been a "companion" to Miss Marchmont. And,
instead of being pleased to have a chance to penetrate a lover's
heart, she resents Paulina's showing off Dr. John's letters,
deeming it the "egotism" in lovers (520). In a word, Lucy is
too emotionally involved to be a "voyeur" any longer. Consequently, the narrative becomes more and more focused on her.

Fewer "irrelevant" episodes or new faces emerge in the second and third volumes. Those who do show up, as in the chapters titled "Malevola" and "Old and New Acquaintance," appear more in the heroine's white-hot fantasy than in real life, because her eyes are "drugged" or charmed. When Lucy shrieks at Madame Beck, "in your hand there is both chill and poison. You envenom and you paralyze," and thinks "she was *my* rival, heart and soul" (544), she becomes a frenzied woman in whom the formerly reserved onlooker is no longer recognizable. Lucy might be speaking metaphorically about "chill and poison," but still she has lost her more objective estimation of Madame Beck. No matter how that lady manipulates for her own interest or dislike the idea of her cousin Paul marrying a poor English girl, it is simply not in her character to plan her own marriage with him without his encouragement, or to play the part of an amorous "rival" too enthusiastically. And furthermore, the narrated events never truly bear out these suspicions of Lucy the character. The scene she beholds in the enchanted garden during her somnambulistic outing also turns out not to be what she has thought. Feverishly persuading herself to welcome the gloomy "Truth" of the supposed engagement of Paul and a young girl (565–566), our heroine, caught in her romantic passions, becomes a drastic misreader of signs.

The thematic resistance to romantic love, of course, can be traced from the very beginning of the novel. Lucy the young spectator once muses, critically, over the part of the "doll-wife" Polly is playing: "One would have thought the child had no mind or life of her own, but must necessarily live, move, and have her being in another: now that her father was taken from her, she nestled to Graham, and seemed to feel by his feelings: to exist in his existence" (83). Later, with the emotionally trapped Lucy struggling to keep in sight the spectator's view of an imperfect John Graham, and criticizing his "cruel vanity" and "masculine self-love" (272), the more sedate narrator warns herself not to "degenerate" "from the faithful narrator . . . into the partial eulogist" (272). A more self-conscious rejection of the persistent romantic longing comes with Lucy's ritualistic burial of Dr. John's letters. The old Cinderella program appears to be inadequate: the "magic" of her kind godmother Mrs. Bretton has only conjured up a disabling delusion. The reappearance of the rich and pretty Paulina immediately shatters Lucy's fragile hope. Furthermore, marriage itself is shown to be, as in Paulina's romance, depriving and limiting.[10] Though Paulina, in her relatively favorable circumstance, seems by far less self-suppressive than Lucy, her measured self-indulgence only makes her more an overpowered slave in her unconditional attachment to man. As she did years before, Paulina plays the willful child and bashful maiden in turn to please her father and Dr. John. She buys her emotional satisfaction at the price of making herself a nonentity—love for man is her only need and her only existence. Emblematically, all her children take the look and temperament of their father; she simply leaves no trace in life whatsoever.

Important as such deflations of the Romance are, with her emotional entanglements with Dr. John and then Paul, Lucy becomes increasingly a familiar type of central character—the tormented woman in love. For all his appearance of an antihero, the short, dark, and harsh Professor Paul is at heart a faithful romantic lover. Their intense friendship—with the man constantly teaching and scolding, the woman arguing and retorting—strains for something new, yet eventually patterns itself into the old conclusion. In the tritest language, Paul offers Lucy a house (home) as well as his hand: "Lucy, take my love. One day share my life. Be my dearest, first on earth" (591). And Lucy, the wistful girl pining for security, companionship, and happiness, hungrily clings to his love—weird and meddling as its expressions sometimes are—and promises "to do all he told" (587).

While the heroine is overpowered by love and ready to give up herself and her critical insight, the spectator in her more and more retreats into the narrative voice, and makes Lucy the character an object of her disinterested watching as well. Hence the growing distance between the heroine and the narrator. From time to time the narrator invades the surface of the story,[11] addressing her readers,[12] discussing her business of writing, in order to emphasize her independent, separate existence from Lucy the character.

An early example of the narrator's interruptive discussion with "the reader" is found in a passage about young Lucy's leaving the Brettons, which is typical enough to be a representative of its kind:

> It will be conjectured that I was of course glad to return to the bosom of my kindred. Well! the amiable conjecture does no harm, and may therefore be safely left uncontradicted. Far from saying nay, indeed, I will permit the reader to picture me, for the next eight years, as a bark slumbering through halcyon weather, in a harbour still as glass. . . . A great many women and girls are supposed to pass their lives something in that fashion; why not I with the rest? (94)

Here the narrator, in a sarcastic tone, invites the reader to "picture" her life as he/she pleases, and thereby underlines both the freedom of literary imagination and the restrictions it suffers from—since the "free" conjecture of the reader (and the narrator) is inevitably conditioned by preexisting texts and the conventional expectation of a heroine's life. Not infrequently, Lucy Snowe intentionally plays the "unreliable" storyteller that Helene Moglen (196, 199) and Mary Jacobus (43) complain about. The most convincing proof of Lucy's "lying" is her concealment of Dr. John's identity from us readers. First, we should make it clear that Lucy's decision to hide her own identity from Dr. John is not at all "perverse." In the fairy tale structure, which is the cornerstone of such narratives, it is absolutely not *her* part to recognize *him*. Her silence tells indisputably of Lucy the character's unconscious romantic expectation of Dr. John. The delay in revealing the truth about Dr. John is indeed a pregnant gesture, not merely a standard technique used to create a little suspense. The fact that Lucy the narrator uses this technique in a very crude and careless way, without any serious consideration of her own credibility, shows, on the one hand, her refusal to make a story sound "trustworthy," and on the other, her distrust of, and alienation from, the conventional readers. Refusing to share the secret with them, Lucy the narrator seems to classify the readers, along with Dr. John, as "blind" people. This self-highlighting narrative unreliability can be taken as a narrating "action" designed to undermine the credibility of all "stories," of the previous models as well as the present ones, and to hint at a different, but suppressed "reality" or "actuality."

Thus the narrator's attitude toward her own "story" is, understandably, strikingly distant and critical. She exposes its roots, challenges its validity, mocks its trite patterns, and even allows the reader to "cancel" it: referring to her own romantic views of Europe, she says, "Cancel the whole of that, if you please, reader . . . " (117). Even the least "loaded" authorial intrusion will in one way or other point to a different vantage point or perspective, as the following paragraph about Lucy's going to the theater with Dr. John: "And away I flew, never once checked, reader, by the thought which perhaps at this moment checks you: namely that to go anywhere with Graham and without Mrs Bretton could be objectionable" (337). Then the narrator goes on to defend Lucy of the time—the reader's probable conventional reactions are presented to be refuted. However, a different point of view is introduced and the heroine's fluttering eagerness is disrupted. A pause is created in the narrative, and consequently, a distance, which reveals the contemplating, weighing, and manipulating subjectivity of the older Lucy telling the story.

The narrator's increasing impatience with the traditional marriage plot is further made clear in the way she perfunctorily handles the subject of love, especially the final stage of the Paul-Lucy relationship. The chapter "Faubourg Clotilde" gives a good taste of the generalizing and distanced narration. It deals with the climactic moment when the lovers, after all their trials, at last come to a sweet understanding—similar to the occasions when Elizabeth Bennet and Darcy get "lost" in their delightful walk in the woods or Dorothea Brooke and Will stand together "with their hands clasped, like two children" (Eliot 559). But here both emotion and compassionate amusement are curiously drained out of the narrative:

> M. Paul talked to me. His voice was so modulated that it mixed harmonious with the silver whisper, the gush, the

musical sigh, in which light breeze, fountain and foliage in-
toned their lulling vesper.

Happy hour—stay one moment! droop those plumes, rest
those wings; incline to mine that brow of heaven! White
Angel! let thy light linger; leave its reflection on succeeding
clouds. . . . (588)

No words of Paul are related. The scene is presented in the trite
poetic language usually associated with pastoral love—breeze,
fountain, foliage—but gives no fresh, touching impression. The
direct addresses to time and light suddenly switch the angle and
expand the distance. As if being looked at from the wrong end of
a telescope, the heroine's experience appears like some vague, re-
mote, and very transient occurrence. The deliberate avoidance of
lively details does not allow the feelings that are mentioned to be
fully conveyed. In contrast with the vivid descriptions of the
queer behavior of young Polly or the dashing speeches of coquettish Miss Fanshawe, such a mode of narration tells its own
"story" between the lines: it is as if the narrator has lost her interest in the present topic; or, she has decided not to talk about her
genuine experiences and feelings, which are beyond conventional language. Even when she comes to some particulars that
are potentially sentimental, her narrative remains surprisingly
cool, sketchy, and colorless: "I have made him a little library,
filled its shelves with the books he left in my care: I have cultivated out of love for him (I was naturally no florist) the plants he
preferred, and some of them are yet in bloom" (595).

In the passage about Paul's love letters, the narrator's estrangement and elusiveness come out even more arrestingly:
"By every vessel he wrote; he wrote as he gave and as he loved,
in full-handed, full-hearted plentitude. He wrote because he
liked to write; he did not abridge, because he cared not to
abridge. He sat down, he took pen and paper, because he loved
Lucy and had much to say to her . . ." (594). Lucy Snowe never
informs us of the contents of these letters, nor those from Dr.
John, which she values "like the blood" in her veins (327). But
in Dr. John's case at least we are told how she, trembling and
sobbing, speculates about the length and tone of the letter

before she actually reads it. Here we have only repetitious nonsense such as "He sat down, he took pen and paper," or "he did not abridge, because he cared not to abridge." Through a style so impatiently trifling and so incompatible with the sentimental subject it deals with—especially in the light of Paul's coming death—the narrator keeps her distance from the romantic situation. Finding the story once more traveling toward a conventional Cinderellean closure, the narrator switches to an increasingly detached and parodic tone, accelerates the tempo of narration, cuts short the story, and reverses the reader's expectation by quickly bringing about Paul's death.

In a way the final separation of the narrator and the heroine is a "solution" for Lucy's inner schism, for it enables the two conflicting impulses in her to fulfill themselves in different spheres. This narrative strategy reminds us of the author's similar effort in *Shirley*, where she splits the female protagonist into two characters: Shirley and Caroline. That experiment was not very successful, though it did enlarge the scope of female activity through an unorthodox "tomboy" who names herself "Colonel Shirley." Caroline's life is exactly another Cinderella tale, while Shirley, being exceptionally advantageously situated, fails to offer a feasible alternative to, or even adequate comments on, Caroline's life. In *Villette*, however, the conflicting parts form constructive comments on each other, struggling toward something fundamentally new. While the unfolding of the plot gives enough space for the play of the personal romantic passions of the heroine, the narrative voice from time to time challenges and deflates the romance from an outsider's point of view. Significantly, it is the narrator/spectator who has the last word. Lucy the character is again decentered and the novel ends coolly with those irrelevant "other" people: "Madame Beck prospered all the days of her life; so did Père Silas; Madame Walravens fulfilled her ninetieth year before she died. Farewell" (596).

In the first three chapters of *Villette*, little is said about Lucy herself. Yet Lucy's extraordinary aloofness, which often escapes our initial notice, is stranger and more fascinating than Polly's sentimental drama. In several places her calmness in a tearful situation is pointed out emphatically. Why is she so ready to be a "cold" spectator? Why should a young girl like her be so alert to "signs" in life? Something must have happened to her when she was younger. Life must have already displayed to her many tokens and omens. Lucy has vaguely mentioned her "kinsfolk" rather than her parents or family. Probably she had been bereft of parental care since she was very young and had grown used to a comparatively unnoticed, marginal position. Clearly, though Lucy does not have her "plot" yet, she already has a "history"—perhaps a more bathetic one than Polly's temporary separation from her father. It is the narrator's deliberate decision to introduce Lucy as a mere onlooker rather than a cinder girl like Jane Eyre that is under the spotlight. "Unobserved, I could observe" (211), says Lucy, driving the message home that somehow her "invisibility," her "cypherness,"[13] enables her to be "a viewer rather than viewed object" (Lawrence 450).

Then the question follows: why does the narrator stress this aspect—this cool spectator in her? Or, to use the words of Gilbert and Gubar, "Why does Brontë choose a voyeur to narrate a fictional biography?" Their answer is:

> Obviously, Lucy's life, her sense of herself, doesn't conform to the literary or social stereotypes provided by her culture to define and circumscribe female life. Resembling Goethe's Makarie in that she too feels as if she has no story, Lucy cannot employ the narrative structures available to her, yet there are no existing alternatives. So she finds herself using and abusing—presenting and undercutting—images and stories of male devising. . . . (418–419)

Surely they are right, but only partially. In *Villette* it is not only that the stereotypic images and stories are undercut and demolished through the eyes of Lucy the outsider, but that something new and positive is created. Lucy's passive action of watching is not only frequently recorded, but dramatized; the narrator's occupation of storytelling is not merely repeatedly mentioned, but underlined. Thus, beside and behind the Cinderella story of a

poor orphan trapped in a stifling social environment and struggling for a home, a different "story" is looming.

The most urgent question *Villette* constantly raises concerns
"the plan" for a woman's life. Early in the novel, when Lucy has
ventured as far as London, she asks: "What was I doing here
alone in great London? What should I do on the morrow? What
prospects had I in life? What friends had I on earth? Whence did I
come? Whither should I go? What should I do?" (107) The string
of questions is exactly about the "reality" of Lucy's life and its
"plot." Jane Eyre, fleeing from Thornfield, ponders the same
problem: "What do the women do?" (331) Lucy's questions are,
as Barry Qualls points out, expressed through language deeply
rooted in the Christian tradition (75); but they are also very this-
worldly and demand a practical answer.[14] We must not forget
that the Lucy in London who is raising the questions is in need of
her next month's food—if not next week's. Later, when Lucy decides to bury her attachment to Dr. John, she again asks: "what
road was open?—what plan available?" (381). Coming from an
anguished woman who is looking at an uncertain future with
painful longing and bleak expectations, such questions sound a
bitter protest against her barren and restricted life. Yet, at the
same time we can discern in them the calmer voice of the storyteller who is meditating on the possible new plot ("plan") for her
heroine.

This quest for the new plot in Brontë's texts is, as I have suggested before, identical with the narrative struggle toward "the
real." If we look back at Lucy's double writing in answering Dr.
John's letter, we realize that neither her suppressed letter nor the
one actually sent represents the "truth" about Lucy. Even the
two letters together do not constitute "the truth," since in them
both her passion and her reason are encoded in her romantic plot,
which we know well will lead her nowhere. "The truth," if we
take her double writing as an index to the "message" of the book,
is the existence of the two letters and the negation of both of them
through Lucy's metaphorical burial of her love for Dr. John.

The search for another "plan" is also carried out through Lucy
the spectator's attentive observation and evaluation of the images
of women she encounters, in life or in art works. She seems to be

surrounded by impossible role models. She cannot and would not be a Paulina, the romantic child/lover and the angel of the house. She will certainly not be a flirt like Miss Fanshawe. The two female stereotypes that she sees in a gallery—one is a picture of a huge voluptuous woman titillatingly named "Cleopatra"; the other is represented in a set of four pictures, especially recommended by M. Paul, depicting the life of a pious, obedient wife—equally repel her. The few exceptional figures with a positive potential are Madame Beck and the actress staging the tragedy of Vashti, the proud, rebellious queen. As a single woman fighting for a position in an alien society, Lucy does not miss the similarity between her situation and Madame Beck's. Notably, when she plans for a independent future, she takes into consideration Madame Beck's example (450) and eventually becomes a school directress. The actress's performance she finds to be even more engrossing and stimulating. Looking at her, Lucy is drawn out of her "wonted orbit" (340) and totally forgets herself. When she gathers that Dr. John assesses the actress "as a woman, not an artist," she is nettled: "it was a branding judgment" (342). The experience proves to be crucial. In the inspired presentation of Vashti she sees the exciting possibility of a female artist creating a new image of woman. As Lucy says: "That night [in the theater] was . . . marked in my book of life . . . with a deep-red cross" (342).

It is through such close examination of the existing models that Lucy the spectator gropes her way toward a new ending. From the very beginning, young Lucy's looking on is not spoken of as an act of childish curiosity, but in terms of literary work. Talking about Polly's leaving, Lucy says: "I was not long allowed the amusement of this study of character" (87). "Study of character"! The connection between idle watching and artistic creation is consciously suggested, to be further realized through the narrative. The "new" solution aspired after is perhaps best manifest through the frequent intrusion of the older Lucy, who is telling her story and insisting on her own separate existence. This awkwardly stressed fact that the Lucy speaking is a writer, an unmarried professional woman, implies a different kind of personal drama—the drama of a marginalized spectator growing into an author. This second "story," of which perhaps Brontë was not fully aware and which yet lacks an established and recognizable pattern, is actually the more important theme of the novel. It is the embryo of a new "plan": the making of a self-exiled artist as a young woman.

By excluding the future embodied by a husband (whether in the person of a Dr. John or a M. Paul), the narrator places Lucy, the wavering and struggling girl, on the road leading toward artistic creation. Things happen in *Villette*, as in many other works by women, in a strikingly arbitrary way. The moment Lucy discovers a new world in the dramatic performance, our long-absent baby girl Polly shows up, as if especially for the purpose of disrupting Lucy's love for John Graham and deflating the conventional romantic plot. Likewise, when M. Paul is on his voyage home to make Lucy just another wife, a storm rises and takes care of him forever. Furthermore, the narrator refuses to make Paul's death a definite fact:

> Here pause: pause at once. There is enough said. Trouble no quiet, kind heart; leave sunny imaginations hope. Let it be theirs to conceive the delight of joy born again fresh out of great terror, the rapture of rescue from peril, the wondrous reprieve from dread, the fruition of return. Let them picture union and a happy succeeding life. (596)

The narrator seems to be reminding us that she might envision a "happy succeeding life" as well as the disastrous sudden death of the lover/hero; it is her own choice that M. Paul should never come back to her narrative to actualize that hollow "happily-ever-after."

With the power of the storyteller thus stressed, the novel, no longer a reliable "true" record of Lucy's life, becomes self-consciously a narrative game, the continuation of the imaginative experiment with the plot for women that young Charlotte began with her Angrian stories. With the privilege of an experimenter, the narrator puts her heroine into all kinds of situations, without trying to make them "realistic." The devices of the traditional romance (the timely rescue from the foreign ruffians in Villette by John Graham Bretton) are freely used; Gothic elements (e.g., the mysterious nun) are drawn in and then casually explained away. The narrator becomes at once the extension of Lucy the heroine and her creator. As the creator, she is the surrogate fiction writer who wants to, by accentuating her "freedom" in spinning a story, make it clear that the forfeit of Lucy's expected marriage is the narrative choice made by the writer, whether out of her gloomy "realistic" estimation of woman's fate in the given society or out of a determined search for a plot beyond the domestic happiness that crowns every romance. As the extension of the heroine—the older, more mature Lucy who is telling the story of her past—the narrator is living testimony that the silent, spectating outsider has eventually gained a voice and found a way to an active life. The evaporation of the hope of marriage no longer necessarily means being buried alive for a woman. It is, on the contrary, a starting point, though a painful one, toward the creation of a new self.

In this sense, the somber ending of *Villette* is not a tragic frustration, but a kind of triumph. A double liberation from the crystallized patterns of conventional language is achieved. The yearning woman breaks the bond of the religious or secular discourses of self-supervision and gives in to her wild passions; at the same time, the spectator/narrator manages, through the half-nostalgic, half-impatient parodic rendering of the last phase of the Lucy-Paul affair, to say a final "no" to the old Cinderella plot. If women still have a long way to go in life and in literature to develop a really fulfilling "plan," at least Charlotte Brontë has won a partial verbal victory in *Villette*, by stretching, twisting, and finally breaking up the inherited narrative pattern, and by introducing into the novel a new type of heroine—a spectator/narrator.

Epilogue:
Beyond Cinderella

With her fascinating presentation of the politics of watching, Charlotte Brontë has touched upon a larger social and cultural issue. In *Discipline and Punish* Foucault uses "panopticism" as a central trope for the structure of the social powers and human knowledges within the modern bourgeois society (195–228). In *Villette*, similarly, all ruling force is related to "gazing" and "scrutinizing," be it Madame Beck's "administrative" (135) control, or Paul's male intellectual authority. Several times the text even suggests a "higher" watching position—for example, through phrases such as "watch-tower" (138) or "watching over" (453)—which anticipates Foucault's notion of the privileged position of the inspection tower in the panoptical system. Even Lucy's quiet looking-on betokens a power—at least, an effort to gain power. Foucault has suggested the relationship between panopticism and individualism, though without further elaboration, when he says that panopticism as an event in the history of the human mind is a special phenomenon of a society "in which the principal elements are . . . on the one hand, *private individuals* and, on the other, the state . . ." (216, my emphasis). In relation to the individuals, "panopticism" as a trope can apply both to the state-individual relationship (in which, as Foucault shows us, each person is viewed by the power situated in the central "inspection tower" as a separate, individualized object), and to the individualistic perception, since in modern Western culture all knowledge, all perception of the world, entails a focalizing subject, and hence is predicated on a panoptical principle.[1]

As the spectator/"focalizer," Lucy puts herself in the center of a micropanoptical system and becomes the subject that eptistemologically organizes the world around herself. Gazing, as it is emphatically depicted in the characterizations of Evelina, Fanny Price, and Lucy Snowe, is a vital action in, as well as a recognizable symptom of, the formation of a female self-consciousness. Looking at the world as a distinct, morally responsible individual, and propelled by an internal dialogue between desire and self-denial (or, passion and reason, etc.), our silent watcher struggles toward a romantic marriage and beyond. The embryo of a future woman artist is already present when Evelina defines herself as a "cypher" and looks on from her window position with a critical eye. But it is not until Lucy Snowe the narrator consciously depicts her gazing as a preliminary step toward her life's work of writing her "heretic narrative" (235) that Cinderella, longing for a secure, happy home, is finally transformed into an independent, professional woman. With the decisive brushing away of the pending marriage at the end of *Villette*, we see how the energy generated by the desire/self-denial dialectic within the Cinderella theme eventually breaks apart the outer narrative frame that contains this ideological and textual dialogue. In other words, the female subjectivity cultivated and nourished by this narrative becomes strong enough and mature enough to find the plot a spiritual straitjacket. The abrupt ending of *Villette* indicates a general, if still inchoate, change of heart toward the Cinderella plot. The quaint, genteel old maids who inhabit Cranford, and who no longer have any prospects of marriage to dream about, became thinkable as central figures of a novel; while girls with Cinderellean ambition, like Hetty Sorrell, Rosamond Vincy, and Gwendolen Harleth, embody a severe critique by George Eliot of the old narrative pattern. In terms of cultural evolution, the Cinderella "story" (or "history") in the classic English novel (here I mainly mean the novels by women writers) is not, ultimately, a personal *Bildungsroman* pointing toward marriage, but a collective effort of generations, a spiritual relay, whose route marks out a heroic march toward a fully grown, artistically creative female subjectivity. It is, to borrow Spivak's words, a history "of female access to individualism" (246).

It was an arduous journey—a hard-won, yet magnificent victory for middle-class heroines like Lucy Snowe over the dominant gender code that still confined women to subjugation and domesticity. However, as I indicated when discussing Fanny Price's triumph, this victory is also quintessentially ambiguous. As is the case with most successful lower-class heroes in popular stories, Fanny's success is achieved through an ironical "swearing-in" to the social position of her former oppressors.[2] Within the basically unchanged social/moral framework, the ascent and centralization of the oppressed individual necessarily involves a reconciliation and/or identification with the existing power, and hence paradoxically reaffirms the system that the individual rebels against at first. After all, even at Brontë's time, the glorification of the creative self is not revolutionarily "new" or uniquely "female": many male narrative voices had done this before Brontë's Lucy, as Sterne's Tristram Shandy does in a satirical, partially self-deconstructive, partially self-celebrating narrative, or as David Copperfield does in his more "earnest" sentimental autobiography.

Spivak tries to emphasize the limitations of this feminist individualism: "The battle for female individualism plays itself out within the larger theater of the establishment of meritocratic individualism, indexed in the aesthetic field by the ideology of 'the creative imagination' " (246). I believe that by exposing the implicit imperialist bias of *Jane Eyre*, Spivak does not mean to "indict" Charlotte Brontë as consciously supporting "imperialist" activity, but to "situate feminist individualism in its historical determination" (244). For all her prejudiced presentation of the animal-woman Bertha from the colony, Brontë does not advocate colonialist enterprise. Her Lucy once expresses a personal displeasure at those people who send Paul abroad for "an Indian fortune" (565).

The unconscious imperialist assumptions embedded in Brontë's hypothesis of a worthy life are, for Spivak as well as for us, a most striking and persuasive example of how the configuration of the private self is inscribed and circumscribed by the collective and/or interpersonal socioeconomical practice of the time. It is interesting to see how the freedom and new space offered by Western expansion to an author like Brontë, who happened to live in a leading imperialist empire, serve to activate, sustain, and/or transform her narrative about the making of a female self. In *Jane Eyre* both the colonial woman Bertha and the missionary St. John Rivers are extremely important as plot elements, and as allegorical figures, which, forming a contrast or complement, help to define Jane Eyre's self-fulfillment. Moreover, a timely inheritance from an uncle engaged in colonial activities enables Jane's equality and financial independence in her marriage with Rochester, and thereby prolongs the "life" of the Cinderella dream. In *Villette* the author also freely used references to colonialism, though for different purposes. For example, when Paul is no longer needed as a male mentor/lover, he is conveniently sent to the West Indies, thereby making it possible for Lucy Snowe finally to grow into an independent single woman and a writer. It seems to me that the expansion of geographical horizons as a result of imperialism considerably increased Brontë's creative freedom, just as it offered additional choices and opportunities for many English men—and women, too—in actual life. Because of this entanglement and interference of the personal and the social and interpersonal, the idea that the achievement of "free" individualistic subjectivity is naturally the goal and the liberation of all women is but another illusion, an extension of the Cinderella myth.

At least partly in view of the radical criticism of individualism, such as Spivak's, we must consider the reservations about female self-assertion on the part of the nineteenth-century women writers. Lucy Snowe is remarkably ambivalent toward her two major "role models"—the actress who plays Vashti and Madame Beck. She perceives in the proud figure of Vashti "a devil," "something neither of woman nor of man":

> These evil forces bore her through the tragedy . . . Hate and Murder and Madness incarnate, she stood.
> It was a marvelous sight: a mighty revelation.
> It was a spectacle low, horrible, immoral. (339)

Madame Beck is presented, on the other hand, in spite of Lucy's admiration of her, as unpleasantly cold and calculating. Lucy is somehow shocked and perplexed by her masculinity: "At that instant, she did not wear a woman's aspect, but rather a man's. Power of a particular kind strongly limned itself in all her traits" (141). Though admitting that Madame Beck is "a very great and a very capable woman," who "ought to have swayed a nation: she should have been the leader of a turbulent legislative assembly" (137), Lucy rather disapprovingly points out that "interest was the master-key of madame's nature" (136). Repeatedly talking about Madame Beck's "coldness" and her self-serving scheming, Lucy, it seems, wants to stress her difference from "the madame." Intriguingly, similar dislike and unsureness are expressed in Brontë's attitude toward Lucy: in a letter that mentions *Villette*, she calls Lucy "cold"(!) and "morbid" (Wise and Symington 4: 18).

Many factors affect Lucy's attitude toward "the madame": her Protestant repugnance to Beck's Catholic system; a desperate lover's frantic fear and jealousy; and, not the least important, her underdog's distrust of a social superior and oppressor. Lucy is obviously somewhat disturbed and disconcerted by the new kind of woman she sees in Madame Beck, which is very different from the stereotype of the proper lady. Nevertheless, Lucy's deliberate distancing of herself from Madame Beck also reveals a deep-rooted female suspicion of the power and self-assertion represented by "the madame," which is basically a copy of its male origin. If we continue our use of the Foucaultian figure of speech, marginalized women like Lucy are (like many other underprivileged groups in different degrees) ambiguously positioned in the panoptical system. Hard as they try to build their own private moral and intellectual "watch-tower," the oppressive environment never allows them to forget that they are, in fact, locked in the "prison cell" as the object under inspection and regulation. They are never quite at ease as the subject, and their watching is always haunted by an acute consciousness of their double position. This is, in the final analysis, perhaps the most vital, and most enabling thing about "feminist individualism"—that is, it is double visioned and essentially ambivalent toward itself.

A quick look at George Eliot's handling of the Cinderella plot will make this point clearer. Her critical shaft is not mainly aimed at marriage as the narrative closure, but forcefully directed against the egoistic nature, the very pivotal ideology that underpins the plot. Some of her practicing Cinderellas are more "romantic" and naively vain like Hetty, others are more strong-willed and clear-headed like Gwendolen, but they are all selfish and all fall victim, directly or indirectly, to the more predatory male individualism surrounding them. As an oppressed group in a stratified society, where people are constitutionally self-seeking and often oppositional in their interests, these egotistic women in George Eliot's world find self-assertion very frustrating, if not utterly impossible.

George Eliot might be seen as having retreated from Brontë's position, in the sense that she systematically denies her women characters fulfillment—either the emotional satisfaction as in *Jane Eyre* or the painful yet victorious spiritual self-realization as in *Villette*. She does not allow female self-assertion to take its turn and play out its disruptive role in a very androcentric cultural structure. However, George Eliot's stand, like Fanny Price's disapproval of selfishness, cannot be simply read as a reinscription of the patriarchal suppression of the female individual. Because she was closer than any other woman writer to achieving the full stature of a male intellectual, George Eliot's criticism of individualism goes much deeper. She seriously questions the validity of the knowledge gained by the panoptical perception of a subject:

Your pier-glass or extensive surface of polished steel made to be rubbed by a housemaid, will be minutely and multitudinously scratched in all directions; but place now against it a lighted candle as a centre of illumination, and lo! the scratches will seem to arrange themselves in a fine series of concentric circles round that little sun. It is demonstrable that the scratches are going everywhere impartially, and it is only your candle which produces the flattering illusion of a concentric arrangement, its light falling with an exclusive optical selection. (182)

George Eliot even overtly spells out that the little candle represents "the egoism" of a person. With her moral and epistemological attack on the egoistic point of view, it is understandable why she refuses to envision some personal fulfillment as the symbolic solution for problems facing her heroine and the society she lives in. Hence her heavy utopian investment in her tentative vision of the "new." Maggie, perhaps George Eliot's favorite, refuses to come back from her erratic boat-floating as a regular romantic bride. A disruptive, all-devouring flood has to be called forth at the end of *The Mill on the Floss* to reconcile Maggie with her family and society in *another* world. Mirah can only join her husband Deronda in straining for a yet vague and abstract new Jerusalem. Such allegorical "utopian" endings, which so far do not carry enough cultural momentum and social urgency to become another popular myth, demonstrate the *unimaginability* of a genuine "new" program within the realistic world of St. Oggs or Gwendolen's England.

As if to testify to the "dystocia" of the new plot, echoes of "Cinderella" are still vibrant in twentieth-century Western popular culture. Today's Hollywood *Working Girl,* though very much adapted to the ways and styles of the eighties in terms of the form of personal happiness (e.g., marriage itself is no longer so important for the heroine as long as a Mr. Right is secured; and a triumphant thrust into the working world becomes a necessary part of the scenario of success), has not marched very far from Cinderella's starting and ending points.[3] Typically, the first step "working girl" Tess McGill takes toward her grand conquest is, exactly like her fairy tale predecessor, to display herself in the grandeur of the borrowed clothing that denotes class, money, and feminine charm. As Radway and others have concluded, for women of today, as for their ancestors, fairy tale romances still urgently touch upon the problems, tensions, and disaffections in their life (which largely accounts for their continual popularity); yet at the same time, these works deflect or help them cure their anger and desire for change by offering fantasy escapes and mythic promises (Radway 87–93, 157–158; Modleski 14; Rabine 165–174, 190).

Accordingly, many "serious" modern women writers, as Rebecca West notes in her essay "And They All Lived Unhappily Ever After," are also obliged to continue their struggle against the phantom of the old myth that still haunts. Margaret Drabble's young girl, entering marriage after her classical Cinderellean journey, is to be tormented and abandoned by her once-charming "prince." Barbara Pym's quiet, neglected, spinsterish woman may eventually be safely married and prove to be of greater spiritual strength. Jean Rhys's Antoinette-Bertha Rochester is another lonely, frightened orphan, yearning, in a fatal way, for love and security in the person of a husband. After dealing with the multiple crises of the "free women" in *The Golden Notebook,* Doris Lessing returns in *The Four-Gated City* to play with a Thornfield-like triangle, which ends with the young secretary Martha's stalking off with the mad wife, leaving the husband alone in his big mansion. "Free women" like Anna and Molly no longer believe in the marriage plot, but they still live in a world that is very much the creation of the generations of Richardson and George Eliot, and they are tormented by the old cultural split between individual desire and social constraints. That is why Anna Wulf in *The Golden Notebook* emphatically denies that they are a truly "new type of woman." She keenly realizes that even the fact that they are labeled as "new" is a result of women being "measured" with the conventional stereotype of domestic and dependent angel of the house: "They still define us in terms of relationships with men, even the best of them" (4). Despite the various outcome, all these writers are yet busy dealing with the classical Cinderella situations—twisting, reasserting, or lampooning the narrative pattern—which itself pronounces the want of a "plan" completely different from the Cinderellean self-fulfillment.

During my work on this book, I happened to come across a piece of the "true" history of a Chinese woman, which forms an interesting comment on the lack of the "new plot" that I am discussing. It is about a Red Army woman named Zhou Qi-yi. When she was very young, it was arranged that she would marry an idiot boy from a richer family, and she was forced to have her feet bound to fit the pair of tiny shoes sent by her future in-laws. (What a horrible actualization of the trial of the glass slipper in the fairy tale!) Eventually Zhou escaped this devastating marriage by taking part in the peasants' revolution.[4] The sudden twist and actual development of the "story" are perhaps beyond the imagination of most Western feminists, yet for quite a time it was a dominant stereotype in the post-1949 Chinese literature (That this stereotypic narrative pattern is in its way limited and limiting is, however, not the subject of the present study.) The relevant "moral" of the story, if there is one, is that the formation of a "new plot" seems to be enabled more by the reorganization of the whole existential environment, rather than by the "free play" of personal imagination.

Maybe it is our work to rethink and reorganize the order of our world. As I write these final words in the spring of 1989, my country is deeply shaken by far-reaching political turmoil. In light of this, it suddenly became acutely clear to me what I have always vaguely known about my study: before, behind, and all around my personal involvement with the English literature and the Cinderella narratives is the larger "story" of a new round of Chinese encounters with Western culture. Nearly every important event in modern Chinese history—the nineteenth-century Taiping Peasants Uprising, whose religious beliefs were tinged with Protestant Christianity, the Chinese Revolution of 1911 that overthrew the monarchy, the May Fourth Movement seventy years ago, Mao's Marxist revolution, as well as what happened recently in Beijing show us, Western ideas play a vital role in the efforts of the Chinese people to reshape their nation. China inescapably becomes a battlefield where different Western ideas clash with each other and with the old Chinese traditions. Because of the gradual, and mistake-ridden process of transcultural understanding (many Chinese, it seems to me, including both fervent advocates of the Western ways and their fierce denouncers, entertain significant misconceptions and illusions about those magic Western words such as "freedom," "individuality," "equality," "democracy," even perhaps "socialism"); and because of the bitter history of Western imperialism, which originally forced the Chinese into this "dialogue" with warships and opium; and because China is still a poor country with over a billion people (most of them poorly-educated or uneducated peasants), a country which is troubled by natural diasters as well as various serious economic and political problems (double-digit inflation, overpopulation, and even the threat of civil war), this all-meaningful East-West dialogue was, and is, bound to be a long, painful, and sometimes violent experience for us.

In the light of this international cultural confrontation, I have come to a better understanding of my own ambivalence toward the Cinderella theme. I share with the women writers being discussed here the equivocal female response toward this complex and multiedged narrative. But my ambivalence has also another root: it is embedded in my fundamentally multiple and self-contradictory reaction toward the metalanguage, the Western myth of self-assertion (and the related ideas) behind the tale. I am aware, on the one hand, of the positive mobilizing power of such myth for women and underprivileged people in general, especially in a nation like mine whose tradition (from Confucianism to Mao's version of socialism) have never undergone a process of "individualization"; yet on the other hand, I see the race, gender, class roots, and affiliation of this myth, as well as its false promises and social, historical limitations. Caught in tense political struggles and harsh social reality—sometimes even in national crisis like generations of Chinese intellectuals before us—we have to grope and blunder, in thought and in action, striving to both absorb and resist that which is Western, to both dismantle and preserve our own tradition.

Yet we have reason to believe that "rethinking" is an action of "reforming." Since this ongoing dialogue is not quite one-sided, not only carried out energetically by Chinese or other third world people—as some influential post-structuralist and feminist efforts to criticize the Western traditions seem to indicate—it stands a better chance to really make a difference in our world. Perhaps, in the persistent endeavor to change the world, some new plot for women, which not only reaches beyond the old Cinderellean narrative closure of the happy marriage, but also transcends its motivating ideological dialectics, will one day become "imaginable."

NOTES

Preface

1. The full exploration of this cultural paradox will be the subject of another study. Nevertheless, I would like to point out some facts that are relevant to the question: 1) "Madame White Snake," along with other famous Chinese tales, is mainly circulated orally among lower-class people. It has not been "purified" and "authorized" as many Western folk tales have, nor has it been successfully assimilated into high culture. 2) Contrary to the belief of some Western scholars that fairy tales are as a rule comic stories, all of the four greatest Chinese folk tales are tragic ones. 3) Those tales about the attractive animal/fairy woman with magic power are usually recognizable male fantasies. This is especially obvious in P'u Sung-ling's stories, which sometimes have a wish-fulfilling happy ending.

2. These are, respectively, the heroines of *Lucy Wellers* (by "a lady"), Charlotte Lennox's *Henrietta Courtney* (1760), Anne Hughes's *Caroline Asford* (1787), and *Juliana* (1788).

3. In his monograph *The Cinderella Cycle in China and Indo-China*, Professor Naitung Ting has mentioned some "social and cultural" factors that might have affected the fate of "Cinderella" in China. For instance, there was in China, especially among the poor peasants, the custom of the child-wife; consequently, the troublesome stepmother-daughter relationship was much rarer, since the parents could always sell their unwanted daughter to another family as a servant and future daughter-in-law (36).

Introduction

1. According to Mr. Chen Tung Yuan, the convention of binding women's feet might have started in the Dynasty of Southern Tang

(125), a little later than the Chinese Cinderella tale was recorded. Ancient Chinese poetry, however, shows us that even before then there existed a long tradition in China praising the female beauty represented by small, delicate feet.

2. In *The Mermaid and the Minotaur*, Dorothy Dinnerstein has discussed this in detail. Bruno Bettelheim has said something almost the same, though he does not criticize the phenomenon as Dinnerstein does. See *The Uses of Enchantment* 114–115.

3. Bettelheim's reading of Cinderella, for all its insights into some motifs and children's psychological reactions, seems to me lopsided and reductive. Narrowly focusing on some Freudian conceptions and overemphasizing "the girl's oedipal desires and anxieties"(248), his interpretation poses the Western nuclear family as the universe. See also Zipes's critique on Bettelheim (*Breaking the Magic Spell* 160–178).

4. The term "myth" in the present sense is borrowed from Roland Barthes's "Myth Today." According to his conception, "in myth there are two semiological systems, one of which is staggered in relation to the other: a linguistic system, the language (or the modes of representation which are assimilated to it), which I shall call the *language-object* . . . and the myth itself, which I shall call *metalanguage*, because it is a second language, *in which* one speaks about the first." (115). The "myth" proper within this double system, the "metalanguage," is almost equivalent to "ideology," or Bakhtin's "socio-linguistic belief system" (282, 356), or Jameson's "master narratives" (29, 340). I prefer the word "myth" here, as opposed to other more theoretical-sounding terms, because it better marks the fictitious aspect of the related ideological concepts—which were, by the way, once referred to by Karl Marx as "the *illusion* of the class about itself" (65, my emphasis). The term "myth" also better suggests the concrete, tangible form (in which it is encountered by common people every day) and the ambiguity and fluidity that are the built-in qualities of its twofold semiotic system.

5. In a chapter on *The Country Wife*, Eve Kosofsky Sedgwick convincingly demonstrates that in the world of the Restoration comedy of seduction, "heterosexual love" is chiefly "a strategy of homosocial desire"(49), a power game among men.

6. I use the term "Puritan" in a broad sense, more in relation to ethical and literary values than to theological viewpoints. The term "Puritan," though more emphatically suggesting a moral austerity, is here almost interchangeable with "Protestant," because, as Max Weber says, the distinction between the ascetic and the nonascetic

churches of the Reformation "is never perfectly clear" (95). Besides, the English dissenting groups that mostly leaned to the Puritan side were extremely influential in the spheres of ideology and education (Kramnick 208). Therefore, Richardson, the faithful Anglican church-man, is viewed by Ian Watt as a writer within the tradition of Puritan literature (e.g., 85, 222), and the set of moral attitudes he champions is generally called "Puritanism."

7. A character in Congreve's play *The Way of the World*.

8. Although there is some inevitable variation and fluctuation in voice and style, Pamela has basically maintained the unity and consistency of her carefully chosen and strictly policed discourse. I could not find in the text enough convincing examples to support A. M. Kearney's allegation that Pamela has two conflictive voices (81), a point that is also endorsed by Terry Eagleton (*The Rape of Clarissa* 29–35).

9. See, for example, Gilbert and Gubar's *The Madwoman in the Attic*, Chs. One and Five; Mary Poovey's *The Proper Lady and the Woman Writer*, Ch. One; Ruth Perry's *Women, Letters and the Novel*, Ch. Five.

10. This legendary figure had been well known in England since Elizabethan times, and had found expression in, just to name a few, Thomas Dekker's play *The Shoemaker's Holiday* (1600), Thomas Delo-ney's book *The Gentle Crafts* (1596–1600), and William Hogarth's ex-tremely popular series of engravings entitled *Industry and Idleness* (1747).

11. Such a literary and moral quarrel is by no means merely the imagination of the novelists. *Shamela* is one good example of the "ac-tual" polemic, the antagonistic reaction to *Pamela*, and Eliza Hay-wood's *Anti-Pamela* is another. The fact that Haywood soon altered her moral stance after the anti–*Pamela* declaration is extremely fasci-nating. Although this conversion was induced perhaps less by Rich-ardsonian eloquence than by the more persuasive fact that Virtue had replaced Lust as best-selling stock, it was nonetheless a good indica-tion of the existence of the debate as well as the social and economic pressures behind the verbal war.

12. Here lies an essential difference between *Pamela* and *Clarissa*. In the latter, the rape brutally crushes the heroine's potential plot for self-fulfillment, and thus forces virtue to its impossible sublimity. In a sense, *Clarissa* is a novel about the infeasibility of the Cinderella pro-gram within the social world under the joint rule of Harlowe-Love-lace. It is more demystifying and deconstructive toward the bourgeois

myths and ideology in that it brings to light the unbridgeable split between the mythical promise (like the happy ending Clarissa once vaguely hopes for) and the "realistic" possibility. Understandably, therefore, despite all the immediate acclaim the novel received, its plot held much less attraction for the yet aspiring and optimistic middle-class people than that of *Pamela*. And that is why contemporary readers persistently implored Richardson to change the ending. In spite of those failed or fallen female saints that have haunted the novel from time to time, relatively few literary "daughters" follow Clarissa to her heroic death.

13. The term "desire" itself poses a problem, a suspicion. It is highly dubious whether there is such a thing as pure "natural" female desire within human society. René Girard has persuasively demonstrated through his analysis of a group of classical novels how the desires that motivate the protagonists are socially mediated. Lacan, by differentiating between need, desire, and demand, and by coining a very pregnant aphorism that "the unconscious is the discourse of the other" (*Speech and Language* 27), further affirms the mediation of desire as a universal inevitability (also see Lacan's "Desire and the Interpretation of Desire in *Hamlet*," especially 13–14, and *Speech and Language* 31, 106–107, 114, 185–200). Desire, as distinct from need, is always inseparable from ways of satisfaction, which are ever dictated by social life and social language. Patriarchal ideology controls women mainly by formulating and channeling their desires, rather than by merely suppressing them. The Cinderella myth, along with other parables and didactic tales, is an efficient device for such channeling.

14. Robin Gilmour has discussed such historical movements in relation to social manners: "The Restoration is a reaction against Puritanism, and is in its turn challenged by the new sobriety of Augustanism; the dandyism of the Regency is routed by the seriousness of the Victorians, only to reappear in *fin-de-siècle* aestheticism, and so on" (11).

15. Bakhtin's statement that the authoritative discourse is basically monolithic is not quite in line with his overall theory of the dialogic quality of all languages, or his more subtle and complex analyses of the literary texts. It seems more a political denunciation of the authoritative language than a logical inference from his arguments, since for him heteroglossia is a kind of positive value both literarily and moral-politically.

16. In his study on Chinese folk traditions, Wolfram Eberhard mentioned some cases that showed that these four popular tales

("Men Jiang" is translated by him as "Men Chiang," "Zhu Ying-tai" as "Ch'u Ying-t'ai") are familiar subjects and/or motifs in folk songs, paintings, and popular operas (65, 114, 117, 121, 122, 159, 160, 166, 170, 187).

17. The fact that Pip's dream is satirized in the novel does not interfere with my argument, since female romantic fantasy is more often parodied and criticized by both men and women writers. What is important here is that these fairy tale figures, in their different ways, function as the "seed" of desire and generate in the protagonists some kind of self-programming.

Chapter One

1. As Gilbert and Gubar argue, in "Snow White" "the voice of the looking glass" is "the patriarchal voice of judgement that rules the Queen's—and every woman's—self evaluation" (38).

2. This contrast between "innocence" and "experience" parallels the antithesis of country and city. But the latter theme is never elaborated in the novel. The "country" virtue, as personified by Mr. Villars, is merely an abstract concept that has no attraction and very little power to counterpoise the "evil" of the city.

3. In her *Early Journals* we see how Burney, with striking humor and exuberance, repeatedly plays upon the sound, formation, and ambiguous meaning of the word "nobody":

> To whom, then, must I dedicate my wonderful, surprising & interesting adventures?—to whom da[re] I reveal my private opinion of my nearest Relations? the secret thought of my dearest friends? my own hopes, fears, reflections & dislikes?—Nobody!
>
> To Nobody, then, will I write my Journal! . . . No secret can I conceal from No-body; & to No-body can I be ever unreserved. The love, the esteem I entertain for nobody, No-body's self has not power to destroy. From Nobody I have nothing to fear. . . .
> (Troide 1: 2)

"Nobody" here is at once an entity (an imagined somebody), a nonentity (nobody), a bodiless entity (no-body), and the projected image of one's powerless self (Nobody). In sum, with this word, young Burney plays all kinds of games of defining a female self. She even asks pointedly: "but why, permit me to ask, Must a female be made a Nobody?"

(2). Her question can be read in two very different ways. It can mean, humorously in its context, why my beloved Nobody has to be of female gender; yet at the same time it poses some serious doubts about the historical necessity that a woman must be made a powerless Nobody. Burney returned from time to time to this motif of female "nobodyness." For instance, at the beginning of her 1770 journal it is written: "Memoirs/ Addressed to a certain Miss Nobody" (97).

4. Interestingly, Burney's other heroines, Cecilia, Camilla, or Juliet of *The Wanderer*, move through the stories in a more picaresque way. All of them behave not very differently from the beginning to the end. In this sense these novels are less structured and less telling in illustrating a woman's true situation in society. Yet, from a slightly different vantage point, Camilla's ever-frustrated yet desperate endeavor to behave correctly seems to imply that the code of propriety is almost incomprehensible for a truly innocent girl.

5. Lewis has cited in his essay Mary K. Rothbert's model that diagrams "the range of emotional and intellectual responses that can be stimulated by the incongruous," according to which, "as a response to threatening incongruity, fear marshals our powers of concentration and humor celebrates the release from tension" (310–312).

6. Mrs. Selwyn's zeal to emulate male wit, though no doubt rooted in the eighteenth-century male-dominated culture and in no sense a gesture of intentional rebellion, is not quite "an unconscious, left-handed deference to masculine authority" as Straub asserts (27). By openly usurping a male role and being constantly engaged in direct verbal confrontation with men, Mrs. Selwyn is already a "trespasser," a linguistic violator of the codified and institutionalized female submission and powerlessness.

7. In his study of the Bible, Robert Alter uses this term to denote certain recurrent and meaningful scenes. See *The Art of Biblical Narrative*, Ch. Three.

Chapter Two

1. The theme of extramarital love is of continual fascination for Smith. In *Ethelinde, or the Recluse of the Lake* (1789), the heroine has to face the entanglement caused by a very kind and honorable married man; whereas Desmond, the radical and idealistic protagonist of the novel named after him, is deeply in love with one unhappily married woman and sexually involved with another. In both novels, such cases, which are usually regarded as "immoral," are treated by Smith

with understanding and open-mindedness, though she still takes good care to make her central heroines behave "faultlessly" according to the accepted social standards.

2. In the Preface to her last fictional work, *The Young Philosopher, A Novel* (1798), Mrs. Smith unequivocally pays tribute to Wollstonecraft by referring to her as "a Writer" (with a capital *W*) "whose talents I greatly honoured and whose intimely death I deeply regret" (v).

3. Mrs. Smith's strong disgust with their dull, gloomy city house and her ardent longing for the country air are recorded by her sister Mrs. Dorset (Scott 2: 26, 31, 34).

4. Rhoda L. Flaxman closely examines Radcliffe's presentations of the landscape in this novel and points out that the best one, i.e., the "word-painting" of the mountainous scenery near the Castle of Udolpho, is organized by the movement of the travelers, including Emily the heroine (27–29).

5. Descriptions of such "literal" imprisonment are, of course, on the symbolic level epitomes of women's position in the society; as Wollstonecraft notes through Maria's immurement in a madhouse: "Was not the world a vast prison, and women born slaves?" (*Maria* 27).

6. Imprisonment is a recurrent theme in women's literature. For relevant studies, see Ellen Moers's *Literary Women* (115, 131–136), Gilbert and Gubar's *The Madwoman in the Attic* (especially the part on Charlotte Brontë), and Nina Auerbach's *Romantic Imprisonment*, especially Ch. One.

7. This is especially true of the modern Western culture and Western language. In the Oriental patriarchal tradition, say, that of China, which remains an agricultural country with its people basically at the mercy of nature, the conception of nature is in many ways very different.

8. Bettelheim reads "the Hearth" as "a symbol for the mother" (248), and the place where Cinderella may be relatively safe, comforted, and unmolested.

9. According to Propp's analyses of folk tales, "lacking" is considered as equivalent to "desiring" in terms of narrative function. The following is his definition of the VIIIa Function: "one member of a family either *lacks* something or *desires* something" (35, my emphasis).

10. Peter Brooks also emphasizes the importance of the folk tale–like skeleton of a novel: "Somewhat in the manner of the traditional sequence of functions in the folktale analyzed by Propp, ambition provides an armature of plot which the reader recognizes, and which constitutes the very readability of the narrative text . . ." (39).

11. About the "mediator" and the "triangular" desire, see Ch. One of René Girard's *Deceit, Desire, and the Novel*. Roland Barthes has also in *S/Z* noticed that "without the—always anterior—Book and Code, no desire, no jealousy . . . writing becomes the origin of emotion" (73–74).

12. Like many novels that begin by mocking the plot but end by returning to it, *The Vicar of Wakefield* illustrates the harm of such romantic dreams through the deceived elder daughter of the vicar; yet the work eventually reaffirms the plot by divulging that the younger daughter's admirer is the powerful and noble-minded lord in disguise; by the end, everyone is happily settled in a truly fairy tale way.

13. The controversy on this question still exists, especially among feminist critics. For example, Annis Pratt reads "the campaign for romantic love" as "an act of protest" against the matrimony arrangement for social and economical interest and the "profound taboo against feminine sexuality" (41–42). Many others are very wary about the ideological implications of the plot. Mary Poovey notes that such narratives frequently simply ratified the patriarchal ideal of female propriety and "helped to drive further underground the aggressive, perhaps sexual energies that men feared in women" (38). Gilbert and Gubar and Karen Rowe have expressed similar opinions. Ruth Perry more emphatically repeats that such early fictional works "tended to reinforce these patriarchal arrangements, celebrating . . . the sort of romantic love which swept away all vestiges of selfhood . . ." (47).

14. We may attribute this story of resistance to another archetypal pattern—that of Daphne and Apollo, Alpheus and Arethusa, Pan and Syrinx, Zeus and Leda/Io/Europa/Danae, as Annis Pratt does in *Archetypal Patterns in Women's Fiction* (3). But the Daphne pattern has also been fundamentally rewritten at least on two basic points: it is embedded in a "larger" story of Cinderellean ascent, and it is transformed into a fable of female triumph.

15. Charlotte Smith's latent radical leanings became clearer in her later novel *Desmond* (1792), which was written when she "formed acquaintances with some of the most violent advocates of the French Revolution, and unfortunately caught the contagion" (Scott 2: 49).

Chapter Three

1. Jane Austen conscientiously gathered and recorded various comments on this novel from her correspondence, from hearsay, and from the remarks of her family members (Chapman, *Minor Works* 431–436).

2. The social-geographical tension in the novel is, of course, not binary, but somehow triangular. There is, besides Mansfield Park and London, Portsmouth, the world of lower-middle-class people. However, it seems to me that Portsmouth is not quite an independent *symbolic place*. It is a complement to London. If the Crawfords represent the flashy, polished "surface" of metropolitan culture, then Portsmouth, in its noise, disorder, shabbiness, and anarchy embodies the dirtier underside of city life.

3. By this I do not mean to belittle the frontal conflict between Wollstonecraft and the established and/or establishing patriarchal ideologies, but to highlight her *connection* with them. Such connections indicate as much her personal imprisonment within the existing social discourses as the intrinsic self-contradiction of her brand of idealistic individualism.

4. In his book *Horizons of Assent,* Alan Wilde claims that irony is in its essence a complex way of acceptance. See especially his Introduction (1–16).

5. A few more words need to be said about Fanny's final estrangement from the Prices at Portsmouth. It is true that their shabby, noisy, and chaotic life, as seen through Fanny's eyes, can be in a way assigned to the "cliché of the anti-Jacobin novel" (Butler 244). Yet the fact remains that because of the harsher struggle for survival, the Prices are opener and cruder sexists. Often forgotten by a mother to whom "her daughters never had been much" (382) and literally invisible to a drunken father, Fanny is an insignificant outsider even in her parents' home.

6. Paradoxically, by banishing Mrs. Norris from Mansfield Park and making her voluntarily share Maria's punishment, the ending of the novel bestows on her a tragic touch and renders her somewhat more complex and interesting.

7. Julia Prewitt Brown claims in her book, *Jane Austen's Novels,* that "Jane Austen's novels unabashedly assume human interdependence. The belief in independence that plays such a significant part in the masculine consciousness, and hence in our tragic literature, does not occupy a place in her novels" (161).

8. Critics with a different perspective, like George Levine, agree with them in finding that Fanny Price conveys little of the "monstrous" individualistic energy (Levine 41–42).

9. Mr. Bennet's style is closely related to that of the relatively secure and privileged eighteenth-century male satirist.

10. Toward the end of the novel, Elizabeth halfway checks herself, as she is about to make fun of Darcy: "She remembered that he had

yet to learn to be laughed at, and it was rather too early to begin" (Austen, *Pride* 380). Such reflections suggest that Elizabeth now has a more humble and practical estimation of a woman's situation in life.

11. A similar fate is assigned to another voluble speaker in the novel, Mrs. Norris. She speaks loudly and exaggeratedly on behalf of the moral conventions and patriarchal order in hopes of gaining a share of power in the world of Mansfield Park. But there is always a visible gap between her true inclinations and her words, a self-contradiction that is partially responsible for the final calamities of the family and her own expulsion from Mansfield Park.

12. Edmund, being Fanny's chief teacher/protector, is, as Brownstein says, "a sort of a father, as well as nearly a brother" (112).

13. I use the term "problem" in the sense that critics call *Measure for Measure* a "problem play." I think part of its "problem" is that Angelo, the complex, problematic hero, does not fit into the overall comic, folk tale structure of the play. The same is also true of Fanny Price in *Mansfield Park*.

14. As Janice C. Simpson rightly points out, the first false Cinderella is none other than Lady Bertram, the history of whose marriage, rendered in a satirical tone, opens the novel and offers a contrast to Fanny Price's spiritual pilgrimage (26–27).

Chapter Four

1. The "Explanatory Notes" in the Oxford edition of *Jane Eyre* suggest: "For Charlotte Brontë's affinity with the work of Richardson, see Kathleen Tillotson, *Novels of the 1840s*, p. 149, and Janet Spens, 'Charlotte Brontë,' *Essays and studies* (1928), xiv. 56–57" (460).

2. Of all the tales told by Bessie, this is the only one that is recorded in its entirety, and therefore is of special importance as a text that has molded Jane's thinking. Strikingly, this intense, Christian tale is told, or rather, "sung," in ballad form, which has a salient tragic tradition and often offers a vision of life quite different from the happy ending of the fairy tale.

3. It is, by the way, exactly the makeup of the Brontë family. In both the Reed and Rivers families, Charlotte Brontë was perhaps writing her fantasy about sibling relationship—which is also an important motif of the original Cinderella tale.

4. This assertion of mine should, of course, be qualified by the

fact Jane the housewife is also the writer narrating her personal history. However, in *Jane Eyre* the action of storytelling is not as systematically highlighted as it is later in *Villette*. The narrative voice, though distinct, is on the whole well incorporated into the *story*.

5. Taking Jane's departure from Thornfield as the dividing line, Rowe separates the novel into two parts, respectively based on the Cinderella pattern and the Christian plot. The Moor House section is thus viewed by her as the Christian story (" 'Fairy-born' " 71, 85–89).

6. This passion/reason dichotomy in Charlotte Brontë, which is central to eighteenth- and nineteenth-century English culture, has been reformulated and reexplored in recent literary studies. Sometimes it is referred to as a struggle between "blunt bourgeois rationality and flamboyant Romanticism" (Eagleton, *Myths of Power* 4); sometimes, between the "natural" and the "supernatural" (Qualls 52); between "fire" and "ice" (Lodge 114–143); between "the angel of the house and the devil in the flesh" (Showalter 113); or, as Gilbert and Gubar put it, between the docile girl like Snow White and the madwoman of anger and strong emotions. Those various definitions, in spite of their distinct perspectives, can often be transcoded into one another.

7. However, I find difficulty with Eagleton's assertion that Jane's inner conflict is "a fictionally transformed version of the tensions and alliances between the two social classes which dominated the Brontës' world: the industrial bourgeoisie, and the landed gentry or aristocracy" (*Myths of Power* 4). I think this "jumping" from linguistic and ideological tension to class struggle is a crude, and sometimes misleading, oversimplification.

8. Young Paulina watches, too, but only her male protectors.

9. Many critics have noticed this double point of view in *Villette*. Earl A. Knies calls it "the dual vision," which is a kind of combination of first-person view and "the third person type of generalized character sketch" (171–173). John Maynard, in *Charlotte Brontë and Sexuality*, also differentiates "Lucy at the time" and "Lucy the narrator" (166).

10. In a letter to her publisher, Charlotte Brontë acknowledges that Paulina is "the weakest character" (Gaskell 488). But, consciously or unconsciously, this is exactly her intention. Brontë's alienation, like the narrator's, is indicated by the stock and lifeless treatment of the love and marriage between Paulina and John Graham.

11. See *Villette* 94, 105, 117, 121, 168, 228, 235, 266, 273, 325, 334, 427, 436, 532, 579.

12. The problem of the frequently referred to "reader" in *Villette*

is not, of course, a simple one. Brenda R. Silver maintains that there are actually "two readers"—the picky conventional reader (most likely male), and the "rebellious" one who is more sympathetic with the narrator (94). I do not argue with this. However, I think the narrator's attitude toward the implied reader remains ambivalent to the end. There is not enough evidence in the text to support Silver's point that the first type of reader is gradually transformed into the second, and therefore enjoys a more cordial relationship with the narrator.

13. My foregoing discussion of Evelina's window position and "cypher-ness" makes it clear, I think, that I agree with Mary Jacobus that "Lucy's invisibility is an aspect of her oppression" (45). What needs emphasizing is that this is also a state of being that Lucy both struggles against and tries to utilize.

14. Though Lucy from time to time asks Bunyanesque questions like "Whence did I come? Whither should I go?" she is fundamentally different from Bunyan's Christian. The Christian always has "the book" with him, his destination is clear, and his road in a way charted. Whereas with Lucy, her only guide seems to be her dissatisfaction with "the books"—the Bible or the preexistent romantic story—and the plot they have offered.

Epilogue

1. People who are immersed in the Western tradition might think this "panoptical" point of view the "natural" and the only possible way of seeing and knowing. However, if we refer to some other cultures, we can see the possibility of different approaches. For example, traditional Chinese painting is well known for its lack of the "right" perspective; object(s) in the same picture can be depicted from different perspectives, including the reversed (inside out) ones. This peculiarity makes it very hard to decide where the implied "I" (seer/artist) stands in relation to the presented scene. In an article on Chinese poetry, Mei-shu Hwang, following the Chinese writer/painter Feng Zi-Kai (translated by Hwang as Feng Tze-k'ai), names such an approach as "multiple or indefinite viewpoint perspective" and attributes this multiplicity of viewpoints to the implied spatial movement (of the seer/artist) in the flux of time (Hwang 32–34). Such analyses, though very illuminating, are not completely satisfactory. Given the simultaneous way a picture unfolds itself (in contrast, for instance, with a story), it is better to view this quality of Chinese painting as an expression of the multiple, split, and "scattered" subjectivity that is absorbed in, and at the same time everywhere around the scene. In other

words, there is no consciousness in the classic Chinese painter of a unified "self" that is fixedly positioned and definitely separated from the scene (the world).

2. Jack Zipes points out that in the folk tale tradition, which glorifies the triumph of the poor and the young, what is finally changed in the story is the social *position* of the characters, but not the hierarchy itself: "[T] he endings of almost all folk tales are not solely emancipatory, but actually depict the limits of social mobility and confines of the imagination" (*Breaking the Magic Spell* 28). In a sense the ultimate "winner" in *Mansfield Park* is the order symbolized by the estate, though it is inevitably somehow renovated through the changes and vicissitudes of its masters.

3. Leslie W. Rabine closely examines this important change—the inclusion of the female working experience in the contemporary mass-produced romance—and demonstrates its social roots as well as its implications (164–174). She also recognizes that in spite of the changes, the narrative structure of today's popular romance has closely followed "the quest for self-fulfillment through love . . . of nineteenth century high romanticism" (176).

4. Coming from a poor family, Zhou was engaged when she was very young by her parents to the idiot son of a local money-lender. When she was six, her future in-laws sent a pair of tiny shoes and said that they would not accept her unless her feet fit into the shoes. She cried and struggled, but the power of the convention was stronger. Her feet were bound (the traditional Chinese foot-binding process forces the toes and the outside edges of the foot under the sole, and usually results in broken bones). When the Red Army came to her village in the early 1930s, she cut her pigtail and took part in their activities. Her parents wanted to marry her immediately. She cried and struggled, and this time with success. She ran away under cover of the night and joined the Reds. And with her small, bound feet, she covered the legendary long march in 1934–35 and joined her strength in overthrowing one state power and establishing another (see *People's Daily*, Overseas Edition, Dec. 6, 1986).

WORKS CITED

Adelstein, Michael E. *Fanny Burney*. New York: Twayne, 1968.

Allen, Walter. *The English Novel*. New York: E. P. Dutton, 1954.

Alter, Robert. *The Art of Biblical Narrative*. New York: Basic Books, 1981.

Amis, Kingsley. "What Became of Jane Austen?" In *Jane Austen: A Collection of Critical Essays*. Ed. Ian Watt. Englewood Cliffs, N.J.: Prentice-Hall, 1963.

Auerbach, Nina. *Romantic Imprisonment: Women and Other Glorified Outcasts*. New York: Columbia Univ. Press, 1985.

Austen, Jane. *Emma*. Penguin Classics. Harmondsworth: Penguin Books, 1985.

———. *Mansfield Park*. Penguin English Library, 1978.

———. *Persuasion*. Penguin Classics, 1985.

———. *Pride and Prejudice*. Penguin Classics, 1985.

Bakhtin, M. M. *The Dialogic Imagination*. Ed. Michael Holquist. Austin: Univ. of Texas Press, 1981.

Barthes, Roland. *Mythologies*. Trans. Annette Laver. New York: Hill, 1972.

———. *S/Z*. Trans. Richard Miller. London: Jonathan Cape, 1975.

Beauvoir, Simone de. *The Second Sex*. Ed. H. M. Parshley. New York: Vintage Books, 1977.

Beer, Frances. *The Juvenilia of Jane Austen and Charlotte Brontë*. Penguin Classics, 1986.

Bercovitch, Sacvan. *The Puritan Origins of the American Self*. New Haven: Yale Univ. Press, 1975.

Bettelheim, Bruno. *The Use of Enchantment: The Meaning and Importance of Fairy Tales*. New York: Alfred A. Knopf, 1984.

Boswell, James. *The Life of Samuel Johnson*. Ed. George Birkbeck Hill and L.F. Powell. Revised and Enlarged 2nd ed. 6 vols. Oxford: Clarendon, 1964.

Brontë, Charlotte. *Jane Eyre.* The World's Classics Edition. Oxford: Oxford Univ. Press, 1980.

———. *Shirley.* Penguin English Library, 1974.

———. *The Professor and Emma.* London: Dent, 1983.

———. *Villette.* Penguin English Library, 1984.

Brooks, Peter. *Reading for the Plot.* New York: Alfred A. Knopf, 1984.

Brown, Julia Prewitt. *Jane Austen's Novels; Social Change and Literary Form.* Cambridge: Harvard Univ. Press, 1979.

Brownstein, Rachel M. *Becoming a Heroine: Reading about Women in Novels.* New York: The Viking Press, 1982.

Burney, Frances (d'Arblay). *Camilla, or, a Picture of Youth.* London: Oxford Univ. Press, 1972.

———. *Evelina, or a Young Lady's Entrance into the World.* London: Dent, 1964.

———. *The Wanderer; or Female Difficulties.* London: Pandora Press, 1988.

Butler, Marilyn. *Jane Austen and the War of Ideas.* Oxford: Clarendon Press, 1975.

Castle, Terry. *Clarissa's Ciphers.* Ithaca: Cornell Univ. Press, 1982.

Chapman, R. W., ed. *Jane Austen's Letters.* 2nd ed. Oxford: Oxford Univ. Press, 1979.

———. *Minor Works of Jane Austen.* Oxford: Oxford Univ. Press, 1982.

Chase, Richard. "The Brontës, or Myth Domesticated." In *Jane Eyre.* Ed. Richard J. Dunn. New York: Norton, 1971.

Chen Jian-xian. "Woman and the Snake." *Tribune of Folk Literature* (Chinese bimonthly) 26 (1987): 41–44.

Chen Tung Yuan. *The Story of Chinese Women.* Shanghai: The Commercial Press, 1928.

Cox, Marian R. *Cinderella: Three Hundred and Forty-five Variants.* London: Nutt, 1893.

Damrosch, Leopold, Jr. *God's Plot and Man's Stories: Studies in the Fictional Imagination from Milton to Fielding.* Chicago: Univ. of Chicago Press, 1985.

Darnton, Robert. *The Great Cat Massacre and Other Episodes in French Cultural History.* New York: Basic Books, 1984.

Defoe, Daniel. "An Academy for Women." *Selected Poetry and Prose of Daniel Defoe.* Ed. Michael F. Shugrue. New York: Holt, Rinehart & Winston, 1968.

———. *The Complete English Tradesman.* 2 vols. Reprints of Economic Classics. New York: Augustus M. Kelley Publishers, 1969.

Dickens, Charles. *Great Expectations*. Penguin English Library, 1965.

———. *Our Mutual Friend*. Penguin Classics, 1985.

Dinnerstein, Dorothy. *The Mermaid and the Minotaur: Sexual Arrangements and Human Malaise*. New York : Harper and Row, 1976.

Doody, Margaret Anne. *Frances Burney: The Life in the Works*. New Brunswick, N.J.: Rutgers Univ. Press, 1988.

Dundes, Alan, ed. *Cinderella: A Casebook*. New York: Wildman Press, 1983.

Eagleton, Terry. *Myths of Power: A Marxist Study of the Brontës*. London: Macmillan, 1975.

———. *The Rape of Clarissa*. Oxford: Basil Blackwell, 1982.

Eberhard, Wolfram. *Studies in Chinese Folklore and Related Essays*. Bloomington: Indiana Univ. Research Center for the Language Science, 1970.

Eliot, George. *Middlemarch*. New York: W. W. Norton, 1977.

Fielding, Henry. *An Apology for the Life of Mrs. Shamela Andrews*. Berkeley: Univ. of California Press, 1953.

Flaxman, Rhoda L. "Radciffe's Dual Modes of Vision." In *Fetter'd or Free*. Ed. Mary Anne Schofield and Cecilia Macheski. Athens: Ohio Univ. Press, 1986.

Foucault, Michel. *Discipline & Punish: The Birth of the Prison*. Trans. Alan Sheridan. New York: Vintage Books, 1979.

Freud, Sigmund. *On Creativity and the Unconscious*. Trans. Benjamin Nelson Duff. New York: Harper, 1958.

Gaskell, Elizabeth. *The Life of Charlotte Brontë*. Penguin English Library, 1975.

Gilbert, Sandra M., and Susan Gubar. *The Madwoman in the Attic*. New Haven: Yale Univ. Press, 1979.

Gilmour, Robin. *The Idea of the Gentleman in the Victorian Novel*. London: George Allen & Unwin, 1981.

Girard, René. *Deceit, Desire, and the Novel: Self and Other in Literary Structure*. Baltimore: The Johns Hopkins Univ. Press, 1965.

Haller, William and Malleville. "The Puritan Art of Love." *Huntington Library Quarterly* 5(1942): 235–272.

Harding, D. W. "Introduction to *Persuasion*." In *Persuasion*. Penguin Classics, 1985.

———. "Regulated Hatred: An Aspect of the Work of Jane Austen." In *Jane Austen: A Collection of Critical Essays*. Ed. Ian Watt. Englewood Cliffs, N.J.: Prentice-Hall, 1963.

Hemlow, Joyce et al., eds. *Journals and Letters of Fanny Burney*. 12 vols. Oxford: Clarendon Press, 1972–84.

Homans, Margaret. *Bearing the Word: Language and Female Experience in*

Nineteenth-Century Women's Writing. Chicago: Univ. of Chicago Press, 1986.

Howe, P. P. *The Complete Works of William Hazlitt*. 21 vols. London: J.M. Dent and Sons, 1930–34.

Hwang, Mei-shu. "Where Is 'I' in Classical Chinese Poetry? An Experimental Interpretation." *Tamkang Review* 15 (1984/85): 31–47.

Jacobus, Mary. "The Buried Letter: Feminism and Romanticism in *Villette*." In *Women Writing and Writing About Women*. Ed. Mary Jacobus. London: Croom Helm, 1979.

Jameson, Frederic. *The Political Unconscious*. Ithaca: Cornell Univ. Press, 1981.

Kearney, A. M. "Richardson's *Pamela*: The Aesthetic Case." *Review of English Literature* 7 (July 1966): 78–90.

Knies, Earl A. *The Art of Charlotte Brontë*. Athens: Ohio Univ. Press, 1969.

Kramnick, Isaac. "Children's Culture and Bourgeois Ideology." In *Culture and Politics: From Puritanism to Enlightenment*. Ed. Perez Zagorin. Berkeley: Univ. of California Press, 1980.

Lacan, Jacques. "Desire and the Interpretation of Desire in *Hamlet*." In *Literature and Psychoanalysis*. Ed. Shoshana Felman. Baltimore: The Johns Hopkins Univ. Press, 1982.

———. *Speech and Language in Psychoanalysis*. Trans. Anthony Wilden. Baltimore: The Johns Hopkins Univ. Press, 1981.

Lauretis, Teresa de. "Feminist Studies/Critical Studies: Issues, Terms, and Context." In *Feminist Studies/Critical Studies*. Ed. Teresa de Lauretis. Bloomington: Indiana Univ. Press, 1986.

Lawrence, Karen. "The Cypher: Disclosure and Reticence in *Villette*." *Nineteenth-Century Literature* 42 (1987/88): 448–466.

Lessing, Doris. *The Golden Notebook*. New York: Bantam Books, 1981.

Levine, George. *The Realistic Imagination: English Fiction from Frankenstein to Lady Chatterley*. Chicago: Univ. of Chicago Press, 1981.

Lewis, Paul. "Mysterious Laughter: Humor and Fear in Gothic Fiction." *Genre* 14 (1981): 309–327.

Lodge, David. "Fire and Eyre: Charlotte Brontë's War of Earthly Elements." In *Language of Fiction*. London: Rutledge & Kegan Paul, 1966.

Marlowe, Christopher. *The First Part of Tamburlaine the Great*. In *The Complete Plays*. Penguin English Library, 1969.

Martin, Robert Bernard. *The Accents of Persuasion: Charlotte Brontë's Novels*. New York: Norton, 1966.

Marx, Karl, and Frederick Engels. *The German Ideologies.* Ed. C. J. Arthur. New York: International Publishers, 1970.

Maynard, John. *Charlotte Brontë and Sexuality.* Cambridge: Cambridge Univ. Press, 1984.

Miller, Nancy K. "Emphasis Added: Plots and Plausibilities in Women's Fiction." *PMLA* 96 (1981): 36–48.

Milton, John. *Paradise Regained.* In *The Portable Milton.* Ed. Douglas Bush. New York: The Viking Press, 1949.

Modleski, Tania. *Loving with a Vengeance: Mass-Produced Fantasies for Women.* Hamden: Archon Books, 1982.

Moers, Ellen. *Literary Women.* New York: Oxford Univ. Press, 1985.

Moglen, Helene. *Charlotte Brontë: The Self Conceived.* New York: Norton, 1976.

Moler, Kenneth L. "The Two Voices of Fanny Price." In *Jane Austen: Bicentenary Essays.* Ed. John Halperin. Cambridge: Cambridge Univ. Press, 1975.

Morgan, Susan. "The Promise of *Mansfield Park.*" In *Jane Austen's Mansfield Park.* Ed. Harold Bloom. New York: Chelsea House Publishers, 1987.

Opie, Iona and Peter, eds. *The Classic Fairy Tales.* London: Oxford Univ. Press, 1974.

Perrault, Charles. "Cinderella: or, The Little Glass Slipper." In *The Classic Fairy Tales.* Ed. Iona and Peter Opie. London: Oxford Univ. Press, 1974.

Perry, Ruth. *Women, Letters & the Novel.* New York: AMS Press, 1980.

Poovey, Mary. *The Proper Lady and the Woman Writer.* Chicago: Univ. of Chicago Press, 1984.

Pratt, Annis. *Archetypal Patterns in Women's Fiction.* Bloomington: Indiana Univ. Press, 1981.

Propp, V. *Morphology of the Folktale.* Ed. Louis A. Wagner. 2nd ed. Austin: Univ. of Texas Press, 1968.

Qualls, Barry V. *The Secular Pilgrims of Victorian Fiction: Novel as Book of Life.* Cambridge: Cambridge Univ. Press, 1982.

Rabine, Leslie W. *Reading the Romantic Heroine.* Ann Arbor: Univ. of Michigan Press, 1985.

Radcliffe, Ann. *The Mysteries of Udolpho.* Oxford: Oxford Univ. Press, 1980.

Radway, Janice A. *Reading the Romance: Women, Patriarchy, and Popular Literature.* Chapel Hill: Univ. of North Carolina Press, 1984.

Richardson, Samuel. *Clarissa, or, the History of a Young Lady.* Penguin Classics, 1985.

——— *Pamela, or Virtue Rewarded.* New York: W. W. Norton, 1958.

Rigby, Elizabeth. "An Unsigned Review in *Quarterly Review,* December 1848." In *The Brontës: The Critical Heritage.* Ed. Miriam Allott. London: Routledge & Kegan Paul, 1974.

Rowe, Karen E. " 'Fairy-born and Human-bred': Jane Eyre's Education in Romance." In *The Voyage In: Fictions of Female Development.* Ed. Elizabeth Abel et al. Hanover and London: Univ. Press of New England, 1983.

——— "Feminism and Fairy Tales." *Women Studies* 6 (1979): 237–257.

Scott, Sir Walter. *Biographical Memoirs of Eminent Novelists and Other Distinguished Persons.* 2 vols. Freeport, N.Y.: Books for Libraries Press, 1972.

Scrutton, Mary. "Bourgeois Cinderellas." *Twentieth Century* 155 (1954): 351–363.

Sedgwick, Eve Kosofsky. *Between Men: English Literature and Male Homosocial Desire.* New York, Columbia Univ. Press, 1985.

Showalter, Elaine. *A Literature of Their Own.* Princeton, N.J.: Princeton Univ. Press, 1977.

Silver, Brenda R. "The Reflecting Reader in *Villette.*" In *The Voyage In: Fictions of Female Development.* Ed. Elizabeth Abel et al. Hanover and London: Univ. Press of New England, 1983.

Simons, Judy. *Fanny Burney.* London: Macmillan, 1987.

Simpson, Janice C. "Fanny Price as Cinderella: Folk and Fairy-tale in *Mansfield Park.*" *Persuasion* 16 (1987), no. 9: 25–30.

Smith, Charlotte: *Emmeline, the Orphan of the Castle.* London: Oxford Univ. Press, 1971.

———. *The Young Philosopher, A Novel.* 4 vols. New York: Garland Publishing, Inc., 1974.

Spacks, Patricia Meyer. *Imagining a Self: Autobiography and Novel in Eighteenth-Century England.* Cambridge: Harvard Univ. Press, 1976.

Spens, Janet. "Charlotte Brontë." *Essays and Studies* 14 (1928): 56–57.

Spivak, Goyatri Chakravorty. "Three Women's Texts and a Critique of Imperialism." *Critical Inquiry* 12 (1985): 243–261.

Stone, D. Donald. *The Romantic Impulse in Victorian Fiction.* Cambridge: Harvard Univ. Press, 1980.

Straub, Kristina. *Divided Self: Fanny Burney and Feminine Strategy.* Lexington: Univ. Press of Kentucky, 1987.

Tanner, Tony. "Introduction to *Mansfield Park.*" In *Mansfield Park.* Penguin English Library, 1966.

————. *Jane Austen*. London: Macmillan Education, 1986.

Tillotson, Kathleen. *Novels of the 1840s*. Oxford: Clarendon Press, 1956.

Ting, Naitung. *The Cinderella Cycle in China & Indo-China*. Helsinki: Academia Scientiarum Fennica, 1974.

Tolstoy, Lev N. *War and Peace*. Trans. Rosemary Edmonds. New York: Green House, 1982.

Tompkins, J.M.S. *The Popular Novel in England: 1770–1800*. Lincoln: Univ. of Nebraska Press, 1961.

Trilling, Lionel. "*Mansfield Park*." In *Jane Austen: A Collection of Critical Essays*. Ed. Ian Watt. Englewood Cliffs, N.J.: Prentice-Hall, 1963.

Troide, Lars, E., ed. *The Early Journals and Letters of Fanny Burney*. Oxford: Clarendon Press, 1988–

Utter, Robert Palfrey, and Gwendolyn Bridges Needham. *Pamela's Daughters*. New York: Macmillan, 1936.

Wain, John, ed. *Fanny Burney's Diary*. London: The Folio Society, 1961.

Waley, Arthur. "The Chinese Cinderella Story." *Folklore* 58 (1947): 226–238.

Wardle, Ralph M., ed. *Collected Letters of Mary Wollstonecraft*. Ithaca: Cornell Univ. Press, 1979.

Watt, Ian. *The Rise of the Novel*. Berkeley: Univ. of California Press, 1967.

Weber, Max. *The Protestant Ethic and the Spirit of Capitalism*. Trans. Talcott Parsons. New York: Scribner, 1958.

West, Rebecca. "And They All Lived Unhappily Ever After." *TLS* (July 26,1974): 779.

Wilde, Alan. *Horizons of Assent: Modernism, Postmodernism, and the Ironic Imagination*. Baltimore: The Johns Hopkins Univ. Press, 1981.

Wise, T. J., and John A. Symington, eds. *The Brontës: Their Lives, Friendships, and Correspondence*. 4 vols. Oxford: Shakespeare Head, 1932.

Wolff, Cynthia Griffin. *Samuel Richardson and the Eighteenth Century Puritan Character*. Hamden, Conn.: The Shoe String Press, 1972.

Wollstonecraft, Mary. *Maria, or the Wrongs of Woman*. New York: Norton, 1975.

————. "Review of Charlotte Smith's Novel *Emmeline*." *Analytical Review* 1 (July 1788): 327–333.

———— *Vindication of the Rights of Woman*. Penguin English Library, 1982.

Woolf, Virginia. "Fanny Burney's Half-Sister." In *Granite & Rainbow*. New York: Harcourt Brace Jovanovich, 1975.

Wordsworth, William. "Lines Composed a Few Miles Above Tintern Abbey." In *The Norton Anthology of Poetry*. Rev. ed. New York: Norton, 1975.

Working Girl. Dir. Mike Nichols. USA, 1988.

Zipes, Jack. *Breaking the Magic Spell*. Austin: Univ. of Texas Press, 1979.

———. *Fairy Tales & the Art of Subversion*. New York: Wildman Press, 1983.

INDEX